THE
AMERICAN
FARMHOUSE

OTHER BOOKS BY HENRY J. KAUFFMAN

American Copper & Brass
The American Fireplace: Chimneys, Mantel Pieces, Fireplaces & Accessories
The American Pewterer: His Techniques and His Products
Andirons & Other Fireplace Accessories
Early American Gunsmiths, 1650–1850
Pennsylvania Dutch American Folk Art
The American Silversmith, His Techniques and His Products
The Pennsylvania-Kentucky Rifle
The American Ax
Early American Copper, Brass, and Tin
Early American Ironware, Cast and Wrought

THE AMERICAN FARMHOUSE.

TEXT AND PHOTOGRAPHS BY

HENRY J. KAUFFMAN

FLOOR PLANS BY TOM CALLAHAN

Hawthorn Books, Inc.
Publishers / NEW YORK

Library of Congress Catalog Card Number: 75–5036
ISBN: 0–8015–0220–9
1 2 3 4 5 6 7 8 9 10

Contents

v

106784

Acknowledgments

Many kind people have guided me to interesting farmhouses, and others have allowed me to view the interiors of their houses. I would like to thank the following people, all of whom have contributed to the publication of this book:

Jay Anderson, Edwin Battison, Raymond Beecher, Helen Belknap, John Bivins, Miriam Blood, Kenneth Brenner, Mary Bristow, Tom Callahan, Lucile Carter, Helen Cupp, Jane B. Davies, Mrs. Hiram Ely, Catherine Frangiamore, Shelby Frazier, W. H. Harrison, Robert Hill, Jr., Caroll Hopf, Cleon Hopkins, Charles Hummel, Dard Hunter, Donald Hutslar, and Roy Johnson.

Also, Joe Kindig III, Benjamin Levy, Nina Little, A. E. MacLaughlin, Sybil McRay, Leland Meyer, John Milner, Robert Mohr, Murray Nelligan, Jerry Lee Pacquin, Harold Peterson, Frances Phipps, Harry Rinker, Willis Rivinus, Parke Rouse, Jr., John Schlebecker, Frank Schmidt, Jacqueline Taylor, M. W. Thomas, William Watson, Peter Wilcox, and Conrad Wilson.

I would also like to thank the following:

The Chester County (Pennsylvania) Historical Society, the Greene County (New York) Historical Society, the Lancaster County (Pennsylvania) Historical Society, and the York County (Pennsylvania) Historical Society.

Introduction

Generally speaking, a farm consists of a plot of ground along with a house, a barn, and outbuildings. The plot of land might range from 55 acres, as on a small New England farm, to 2,000 acres on a large Virginia plantation. In 1868 there were 2,033,665 farms including 405,280,851 acres in the United States, showing an average of 199 acres for each farm. Certainly one reason for focusing on farmhouses is their preponderance in North America. For many years farming was the leading occupation in the United States, as evidenced by the fact that the highest proportion of the gross national income derived from agricultural products and that the greatest part of the nation's population was engaged in their production. At the turn of the nineteenth century, 95 percent of the population was involved with some aspect of farming. At the turn of the twentieth century, farming continued to compete with manufacturing in importance. By 1965, however, the majority of our population had been attracted to the cities and their outlying suburbs, where employment and conveniences were more plentiful and life seemed less rigorous.

Today, however, the farm is again casting its spell, luring many people back to live in the country or, when this is impractical, to visit it frequently and experience the compensations that country living has to offer.

One of the most interesting discoveries made in this survey of the American farmhouse is that many farmhouses, despite their present ample proportions, were initially small. As a family outgrew their original homestead and as financial circumstances permitted, additions of one kind or another were made. In some cases accommodations for hired help were required; in others, the addition of a new wing provided a married son and his bride with a separate domicile. Sometimes a new house was built nearby, rather than an addition to the old house. This procedure was invariably preferable, since often the addition was made in a style that was not compatible with the style of the existing structure, thereby destroying the unity of the buildings.

Many farmsteads became a family's heritage, with ownership passing from one generation to the next. Except for the movement westward there was little mobility in farm life. While interviewing owners of interesting farmhouses, I met one woman who had never been more than twenty miles from the place of her birth. Farmsteads often became cherished legacies, enriching the lives of generation after generation. And if the chain of ownership was broken, it was not uncommon for a later generation to repurchase the farm, renovate it, and "live happily ever after."

It also becomes evident in this survey that each ethnic group built houses consistent with its background and traditions. Settlers in Massachusetts and Virginia mirrored their structures after those in which they had lived in England, while early settlers in the Hudson River Valley built domiciles such as they had known in the Netherlands. However, there were a few exceptions to this rule. The Germans in Pennsylvania did not build their houses and barns under one roof, as was customary in their native country. And their departure from an earlier tradition still remains unexplainable.

Possibly the most important sociological aspect of farmhouses is the fact that they formed the nuclei of daily family life. Instead of each member of the family "taking off" on his separate way, as is done today, entire families spent much of their time together. During the day family chores were scattered throughout different areas of the house and barn, but at night most of the family activity centered around a fireplace. There the children learned many simple household arts, while their parents engaged in more difficult operations, such as tailoring, quilting, and repairing shoes.

The various outbuildings connected with farmhouse activity were constructed as extensions of the farmhouse, each designed to perform a particular function of farming activity that could be done more effectively outside the main house. Few have serious architectural appeal, yet their very simplicity evokes an indefinable charm. Today, in most cases, they have been destroyed or allowed to collapse; those which survive add immeasurably to the aesthetic aura of a farm.

Large and historically important houses are not emphasized in this book, since most farmers were a part of the extensive "middle class," and their home reflected their income. Some very modest farmhouses have been included, as have a few very elaborate ones. However, it will become evident from the houses included herein that most farmers lived comfortably. Also, it would have been an impossible undertaking to try to cover farmhouses in all of the areas of our vast country, so I have concentrated upon major areas of farming and the houses that were built therein during the seventeenth, eighteenth, and nineteenth centuries. Some of the houses such as the Shirley Plantation House in Virginia, are well known and have been preserved through the years with care; others were abandoned long ago but their weathered frames are of interest in themselves, as they lend presence to the landscape.

It is regrettable that the farmhouse is slowly disappearing from the American scene. The consolidating of farms, plus the crunch of approaching suburbia, are eliminating them rapidly. It is hopeful that the contents of this survey will encourage the preservation of many others.

Part I
NEW ENGLAND

1 Plymouth Colony

Among the earliest farmhouses in America were those built in Plymouth Colony. However, a study of these houses is beset with problems, since none of them have survived. In addition, there is little mention of them in historical accounts, perhaps because they were simple functional buildings, an ordinary part of the settlers' daily lives. Historians have analyzed exhaustively the motivations for colonization—the religious dissent, a need for replenishing a dwindling supply of lumber at home, and the search for a trade route to the East. Now, for the first time, a study will be made of the more mundane aspects of the lives of the colonists, namely, the primitive shelters built by those who reached the stormy coast of New England in December 1620.

One of the first priorities after the colonists arrived was to obtain an adequate food supply. To this end the colonists turned to farming, even though many had not been tillers of the soil in their homeland. It is known that while some had been farmers, others were descendants of farmers, and as a result they were reasonably familiar with the prerequisites of a farmhouse. It was this type of house that they built upon arriving in America. As a matter of fact, most of the early houses built in America were suited to farm life, since, until cities became large manufacturing centers, farming was, of necessity, the major occupation.

Although William Bradford reported some of the colonists' day-to-day activities in his great diary, *The History of Plymouth Colony*, he wrote extremely little about their houses. He comments about their relations with the Indians as well as with their sponsors in England, he discusses their hunting and fishing exploits, and he reflects upon the personal problems that plagued the villagers. Details of house and barn construction, however, seem to be beyond the scope of his interest.

Bradford does mention that strong gales kept the colonists aboard the *Mayflower* for two days after selecting a permanent site, and thereafter men went ashore to "cut and rive timber." Temporary shelters were built, but the first permanent settlement was located on a site that the Indians had cleared for farming (and later rejected) before the colonists arrived. Here there was plenty of virgin oak to build their first abodes. This wood had been used for house construction in England, and it was of the highest quality; it could be easily split, was very resistant to decay, and had excellent color.

Most of the houses built in the first quarter of the century after the colonists landed consisted of one room on a ground floor with a loft overhead and sometimes a lean-to attached alongside of the house. There were no cellars. The large room was called a hall or "great room" and it was rectangular in shape with a large fireplace built into one of the walls.

Recently, however, several Plymouth Plantation archaeologists discovered that another type of construction was used in the first houses built in Plymouth Colony. The *Plymouth Plantation Newsletter*, December 1973, reports this discovery and describes the main features of the house plan:

> Archaeological work in Kingston at a site acquired by Isaac Allerton about 1627 suggested that the early colonists may have used more than one house-type in their original village.
>
> Findings in the dig showed no evidence of the stones under sills that we have used in the village houses to date. Instead there were indications of four substantial holes at what appeared to be the corners of the house. This suggested that Mr. Allerton, perhaps before 1630, had erected a post hole house, a type of construction with which we were vaguely familiar, which was used in the New England Pilgrim times, but for which we had not heretofore found evidence in early Plymouth. [The present reconstruction is not on the original Plymouth site.] The principal feature of the post hole house is that the whole structure is hung on four massive posts buried in the ground for one-third of their length. The remainder of the structure—plates and girts, roofing timber and studdings, are hung on or supported by the four posts. The chimney of frame, wattle and daub construction and the wattle and daub walls between the studding similarly are supported by posts and principal framing timbers. . . .
>
> A dramatic moment in the construction was the day when the principal girts and posts, looking like two giant oaken staples, were raised and slid into the ground by some thirty persons in the same manner as the task might have been carried out in 1620–21.

An illustration of the John Billington house in the process of construction shows the four posts, plates, girts, and studdings in place. For the walls the wattle and daub technique was used; small twigs were woven between the studdings, as shown in the lower part of the chimney. These interstices were later covered with mud, and then clapboards were applied to the frame, leaving appropriate openings for the door and windows (see photos of the Billington house). Because men were shorter of stature in those days, the doors were made proportionally smaller.

The most important feature of the main room was a huge fireplace, built within an end wall. For the first few feet upward from the ground it was constructed of stone, thereafter with wattle and daub, including part of the chimney that was exposed above the roof. Its location within the wall of the house protected the wattle and daub from inclement weather and allowed the small amount of heat radiating from the chimney to be retained within the house. The chimney was also thought to draw better if kept within the walls. The sacrifice of space, otherwise usable in the living room, was the penalty for such a location.

The fire chamber was approximately six feet high and eight feet wide, with a large wooden lintel supporting an overstructure between two jambs. There was no mantel shelf for bric-a-brac, and the entire structure was geared to utility rather than decoration. The survival of fireplaces with wooden chimneys can be partially explained by the fact that a large roaring fire was rarely (if ever) built in them; therefore, the walls did not become too hot. Some houses, of course, did burn down. Crosswise in the throat (the tapering area above the chamber), several lug poles were inserted from which kettles were suspended by a chain, later by a trammel. Since the farmer's wife continually needed hot water, a kettle of water was suspended from one of the poles above the fire. At times these wooden lug poles broke and spilled the contents of the kettles on anyone sitting close to the fire.

Other major uses of the fireplace were for heat and light. Unfortunately, unlike the modern flues, the chimney had no damper; it is estimated that about 90 percent of the heat went up the chimney. One had to sit close to the fire to warm oneself. At the end of very large fireplaces, a bench was often placed for old people to use. This area was called an inglenook. Shallow openings in the jamb walls were used to keep a drink warm, or to hold containers for seasonings such as salt and vinegar, or later, to hold the tinderboxes that were used to start the fires.

One of the major crafts plied by the farmers at the fireside was the spinning of thread. Sheep provided wool, flax provided fibers for linen yarn, and virtually every family had at least one spinning wheel. Looms were relatively scarce, not only because of the cost and size, but also because many hands were needed to supply thread for one weaver.

The furnishings of this one room were few and crudely built. Tabletops and chest boards were split or roughly sawed with a pit saw and often were

An early phase in the construction of
the John Billington house. Courtesy
of Plimouth Plantation, Plymouth,
Massachusetts.

Construction of the John Billington house nearing completion. Courtesy of Plimouth Plantation.

Completion of the John Billington house, showing the small size of the windows. Courtesy of Plimouth Plantation.

View of an interior of a house at Plymouth, showing a typical fireplace. Courtesy of Plimouth Plantation.

Cooks using a table supported by barrels. A trammel, from which a pot is suspended, is in position in the fireplace. Courtesy of Plimouth Plantation.

8

smoothed on only one side. There were few chairs, because a bench required approximately as much work as a chair and could seat a number of people. A bed was located in one corner of the room, usually concealing a trundle bed, which was brought out at night to be used by the children. The table had a trestle base so arranged that it could be dismantled when space was at a premium. Often there was a six-board chest for storage and for sleeping in an emergency. There was no storage space except in the loft and in a lean-to, if the house was so blessed.

The lean-to was often cluttered with objects such as bundles of feathers, broken spinning wheels, a little firewood kept in a dry place, and dried herbs, which were hung from the ceiling. Late in the century objects such as barrels, tubs, dough boxes, and often the family loom were sheltered there.

Pandemonium probably reigned in a few houses, while others were kept shipshape. No two of them were built or furnished exactly alike; some were very comfortably arranged, while others were cold and drafty. By 1650 houses were being built larger, some having two rooms, with a fireplace and chimney built into the middle partition. They were better furnished and more responsive to the requirements of the daily life of a New England farmer.

The original houses were erected within a palisade to protect the residents from marauding Indians and unwelcome wild animals. At one end of the enclosure was a gate, which was opened during the day and closed at night. At the other end, a flat-roofed, fortlike building was erected, the roof of which served as a platform for ordnance, while the main room was used for meetings of a secular and/or ecclesiastical nature. A fence of vertical boarding was constructed around each house to enclose a small garden and a separate grazing area for domestic animals, such as sheep and goats.

Originally, the farming community operated on a communal plan, but it was not many years before some of the colonists protested about this arrangement. Bradford wrote the following account in his *History of Plymouth Colony:*

> For young men who were most able and fit for service objected to being forced to spend their time and strength in working for other men's wives and children without recompense. The strong or the resourceful men had no more share of food, clothes, than the weak man who was not able to do a quarter the other could. If (it was thought) all were to share alike then all were to do alike, then all were on an equality throughout, and one was as good as the other; and, so, if it did not actually abolish those relations which God himself has set among men, it did at least greatly diminish the mutual respect that is so important and should be preserved among men.

Winter scene showing houses within the enclosure at Plymouth. The fence in the foreground is made of wattle. Courtesy of Plimouth Plantation.

In 1623 the Colony was divided in the following fashion:

> Every person was given an acre of land for them and theirs, and they were to have no more till seven years had expired, it was all as near the town as possible, so they might be kept close together, for greater safety and better attention to general employment.

In 1627 another important division was made that was of great significance to the farming community:

> The cattle were divided first, in this proportion: a cow to six shares and two goats to the same, the stock first equalized according to age and quality, and then drawn for by lots. Pigs though more numerous were dealt with similarly. Then, they agreed that every person or share should have twenty acres of land allotted to them, besides the single acre they already owned.

Since there were no exceptions to the divisions of the land and livestock, one can assume that all the families were very dependent upon farming pursuits. Some men may have been largely engaged in carpentry or other trades, but all owned the same amount of land, and it is likely that all were farming and raising the same crops. The economy was too tight to allow land to lie fallow, despite the need for commodities other than food.

One might surmise that some families raised more food than needed, with the result that the excess was bartered at the local exchange for cloth, hardware, tools, et cetera. The storekeeper in turn took the produce to Boston and swapped it for goods, which he and others needed, and which were not locally available. The Boston merchants sent their grain, hides, and timber to the Caribbean, where they were bartered for sugar and molasses, to be sent to England. There the goods were exchanged for the needs of the Boston merchant. These were brought to America and in turn found their way to the local shopkeeper and then into the homes of the colonists. Thus, a four-cornered trade occurred without the farmer going beyond his community.

Corn became the staple crop of the colonists for many years. Every schoolchild learns about Squanto, who taught the Pilgrims to plant corn in hills and fertilize the hill with fish. Corn, however was an alien crop to the early settlers; they yearned for the time when peas and English grains, such

Sheep within an enclosure at Plymouth. Courtesy of Plimouth Plantation.

Harvesting grain with a scythe at Plymouth. Courtesy of Plimouth Plantation.

Pigs within an enclosure at Plymouth. Courtesy of Plimouth Plantation.

as wheat, oats, and barley, could be planted. The problem with these grains was that the ground had to be thoroughly broken for planting, a condition not demanded by corn. It could be planted in small hills broken with a stick or a hoe. However, the elite of the community scorned corn as a food, referring to it as "Indian fare." The gardens adjoining each house bountifully produced most of the vegetables known in their homeland, in addition to pumpkins, squash, and Indian beans, the latter being planted near the cornstalks, which they entwined. Plenty of fruit, such as apples, pears, plums, and cherries, was available from trees.

Although no farm animals were brought over on the *Mayflower*, it soon became apparent that they were needed here. The common draft animal was the ox. The slow, plodding ox was suited to the rough terrain of New England, and after pulling the plow for ten years, they ended up on the farmer's dinner table.

By 1630 Plymouth Colony had 250 inhabitants, some living within, but most outside, the original enclosure. One hypothetical sketch of the village shows that only twelve houses were enclosed by the stockade. By reading *Husbandmen of Plymouth* by Darrett B. Rutman one gets a glimpse of the daily life of the farmer. Rutman describes the implements and procedures of the field and the barn but gives little information about the house in which the farmer lived. One can also visit the reconstructed village of Plymouth, where a number of houses are built within a newly constructed enclosure and are open to the public. A combination of these resources has been used to describe the first permanent houses built by the farmers of Plymouth Colony. Unfortunately, little is known about the barns of the village, and to date, none have been reconstructed for the visitor to see.

2 Massachusetts

By 1640 the lot of the farmer had improved, and settlements were made at some distance from the original site. One of these is the Thomas Plympton house, originally built in South Sudbury, Massachusetts, and now relocated at the Henry Ford Museum at Greenfield Village in Dearborn, Michigan. Plympton came to America as an indentured servant of Peter Noyes and later married Noyes's daughter, Abigail. Plympton is considered to be the founder of the Puritan settlement of Sudbury in 1638. In 1676 he was killed while accompanying a friend on a mission into Indian territory.

The Plympton farmhouse is a simple one-room, one-story, Puritan home, about twenty by twenty-five feet, covered with clapboard. There is a loft which was reached by a ladder standing just beyond the fireplace. The important features of the interior are the horizontal sheathing on the walls, the large central summer beam, and the exposed rafters. Although it now has double-hung windows, the original ones were casements with diamond-shaped panes.

There are two more very unusual features in this seventeenth-century farmhouse. One is the fireplace, which is set lengthwise in the middle of the room and about six feet away from the back wall. This location undoubtedly kept some of the heat in the room, which would have been lost were the fireplace set against an outside wall. The other uncommon feature is a well that is located in a far corner of the house. It is a stone structure enclosed by a wood housing.

At the time this house was built and first used, much of the furniture might have been made by Plympton, when he was not otherwise occupied with his farming activities. Although the present furnishings represent the necessities of family living, they date principally from the end of the seventeenth and well into the eighteenth century. The amount of lathe work in these furnishings indicates that they were not made by an amateur furniture maker. However, the round legs of the spinning wheel could have been fashioned by a man who had only a plane with which to work. All the chairs, the candlestand, and the legs on the dough tray were skillfully turned on a lathe.

The pine dresser is stocked with pewter and woodenware—mostly plates—and a few pieces of hollow ware. The pewterware was probably reserved for Sundays, while the woodenware served everyday needs. The cupboard and its contents were obviously geared for use in a rural household. Pewterware must have been very scarce, since each piece was enumerated in wills and so designated to an heir. The chairs are Carvers and slat-backs.

The fireplace equipment is made mostly of wrought iron; the brass warming pan has an iron handle. There is a small iron kettle on a trivet on the hearth, and another suspended from the crane within the fireplace. Herbs are hung from the rafters as if drying for winter use. Such furnishings are a long step from those used in Plymouth at an earlier time.

Another surviving New England farmhouse of the seventeenth century is the Fairbanks house, which is one of the most important examples. It was built by Jonathan Fairbanks, who with his wife Grace and their six children came from Sowerby, in the vicarage of Halifax, Yorkshire, England. They originally lived in Boston for three years and in 1636 settled in Dedham (then called Contement), Massachusetts.

Fairbanks came from a section of England that lacked good building stone. However, oak was widely available and traditionally used for building houses in England, so Fairbanks brought oak timber along with him, an action that must be regarded as a prime example of "carrying coals to Newcastle."

He split clapboards five inches wide and four to six feet long and left the house unpainted, probably because paint was expensive. Also, oak wood is known to withstand the elements very well. Originally, the roof was covered with thatch, but because of the danger of fire and the hostile climate of New England, it was later covered with hand-split shingles.

The Fairbanks house was built according to what was at that time an unusual floor plan for New England farmhouses—two rooms on the first floor, two on the second floor, with a huge chimney stack between them. The first floor consisted of a hall, which doubled as a kitchen, and a parlor, which was reserved for important social gatherings. Inside the front door and between the two rooms was a small entry, from which one could enter either room of the first floor or ascend the steps to the second floor. On this upper floor were two bedrooms: one was called the hall chamber, and the other was known as the parlor chamber. The massive chimney stack was built off-center, because one room on the first floor is larger than the other.

Such a small house must have provided tight quarters for eight people, along with their farming equipment and tools. As space became cramped, Fairbanks built an addition across the rear, creating what is now known as a

Exterior view of the Thomas Plympton house. Collections of Greenfield Village and the
Henry Ford Museum, Dearborn, Michigan.

Interior view of the Plympton house showing the unusual locations of the fireplace and the wellhead in the far corner. Collections of Greenfield Village and the Henry Ford Museum, Dearborn, Michigan.

Exterior view of the Jonathan Fairbanks house located at Dedham, Massachusetts. Courtesy of the Fairbanks Family of America, Inc.

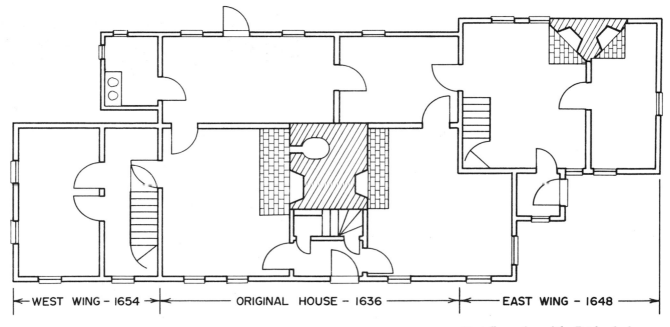

←— WEST WING - 1654 —→   ←——— ORIGINAL HOUSE - 1636 ———→   ←— EAST WING - 1648 —→

First-floor plan of the Fairbanks house.

saltbox house. This addition, made in 1640, provided the Fairbanks with an additional bedroom, a dairy/workroom, and a new, larger kitchen in between. The workroom was probably used to store both farming and household equipment.

In 1648 a wing was added to one end of the Fairbanks house overlapping it slightly, thus elongating the length of the first section and providing an entry to the new section. This portion was presumably built for young John Fairbanks and his bride. On the first floor were a parlor and a bedroom with corner fireplaces in each room, using a common stack. A stairway led to two more bedrooms overhead.

Continual expansion of farm activities required the use of hired help for whom living space had to be provided, and eventually another wing was added to the other end of the house. This wing contained a separate entry and stairs to the second floor to prevent strangers from passing through the main house. However, the hired help had to traverse the kitchen to get to the dairy and workroom. No fireplaces were built in this last wing.

Many features of the Fairbanks farmhouse can be found in other seventeenth-century New England farmhouses, but the Fairbanks house is unique because of its combination of features, such as its great length—175 feet, its brick nogging, the low ceilings and doors, its various partitions, and the winding staircase, leading to the second floor.

One had to have permission to settle in a community, which presumably Fairbanks obtained in order to build his house in 1636. In 1637 Fairbanks was granted a 12-acre lot, 4 acres of which were meadowland. Although this may seem like a rather small allotment, it should be remembered that considerable time was required to clear land and ready it for planting. The inclusion of meadowland is an indication that Fairbanks owned both cows and oxen. Later the same year, he received an additional allotment of 4 acres. The farm eventually reached a size of 150 acres.

Fairbanks died in 1668. An inventory of his estate sheds further light on his agricultural pursuits. His land was divided into six acres of meadowland, two acres of forest, twenty-two acres of upland, and a unnamed number of acres in "Low playne." In addition, many farming tools are recorded, as are crops, such as corn, rye, peas, hemp, and flax. Sheep's wool, a cider press, three swine, four cows, one yearling calf, two steers, and hay were found in his barn, and among the artifacts found in his attic were an ox saddle, candle molds, a pannier, foot warmers, and Dutch ovens.

The Jonathan Cogswell farmhouse was built in the northeastern section of Massachusetts during the first half of the eighteenth century. Extensive information about the houses that stood on Cogswell's grant is provided in a very thorough study of the site and people that was published in *The Historical Collections of the Essex Institute*, vol. XXVI, April 1940. The title of the report is "John Cogswell's Grant and Some of the Houses Thereon, 1636–1839."

The history of the Cogswell houses, or rather the Cogswell grant, begins in the year 1592, in Leigh County, Wilshire, England. In that year a son John

Interior of workroom in the Fairbanks house. Courtesy of the Fairbanks Family of America, Inc.

was born to Edward and Alice Cogswell. In 1615 John married Elizabeth Thompson, and on May 23, 1635, this couple, along with their eight children, sailed for America aboard the ship *Angel Gabriel.*

In 1636 the Cogswells received two grants of farmlands. One of approximately 12 acres was located in the town of Ipswich, and on that site the first Cogswell farmhouse was built. A second grant of 300 acres was located in Chebacco, with boundaries precisely specified by rocks, creeks, and trees. The boundaries of this grant have changed very little from 1636 until the present.

In 1669 John Cogswell died, and due to loosely worded portions of his legacy, the exact site of his house will never be known. It is recorded in *The*

Cogswell Family History that, in 1636, John built a log house on the Ipswich site; however it is likely that this report is an inaccuracy, since in times past historians have been overly intrigued with the use of log cabins by pioneers. For example, in the late nineteenth century an artist portrayed Leyden Street in Plymouth, Massachusetts, as an avenue of log houses; research reveals that no log houses were built in New England in the seventeenth century.

On November 30, 1651, John Cogswell and his wife, Elizabeth, deeded a parcel of land containing 60 acres to their son William. This plot was bounded on the southeast by the Chebacco River, and it is known that upon this ground stood William's barn. This is the first time that there is evidence of a building on the 300-acre grant, and it is now thought that the original house stood where the present Jonathan Cogswell house now stands.

In 1668 William Cogswell was fifty years old. By this time he had acquired his father's entire 300 acres (which previously had been divided) and he was one of the most prominent men in his community. He must have been an active farmer, for in the same year it appears in the town records that he had liberty to "fell timbers" for the end of a barn and for an outhouse, as well as two tree planks for a barn floor, two hundred "Rayles and posts" for a yard by his house, and a tree for stakes and hedging.

For fifty years the 300 acres of the original grant remained intact, but in 1687, as William was approaching seventy, he decided to divide the land as his father had done many years before. He executed deeds for different parts of the grant to legally become the property of his sons following his and his wife's deaths. *The Cogswell Family History* provides the following account:

> Jonathan, Jr., was born in 1687, the same year that his grandfather divided up the grant. He is of special interest to us as we believe that it was he who took down the old house, and built the present one in its stead. Just when this was done we have, at present, no means of knowing, but a careful scrutiny of the chief events of Jonathan, Jr.'s life seems to point to the date 1730. . . .
>
> It seems fair to suppose that after his second marriage, and with the rapid increase of his family, he would find the simple old house of his grandfather, with its crude 17th century interior, too small and cramped. And it seems logical that he would build himself a house on the same site utilizing the same cellar, the same mammoth chimney with its four large fireplaces, and some of the old timbers and boarding, having, however, new fashioned panelling instead of the plain sheathing, and plastered walls and ceilings in place of the exposed framing of the earlier period.

In 1752 Jonathan Cogswell died at the age of sixty-five years. Many papers were filed concerning his estate, including a complete inventory of his

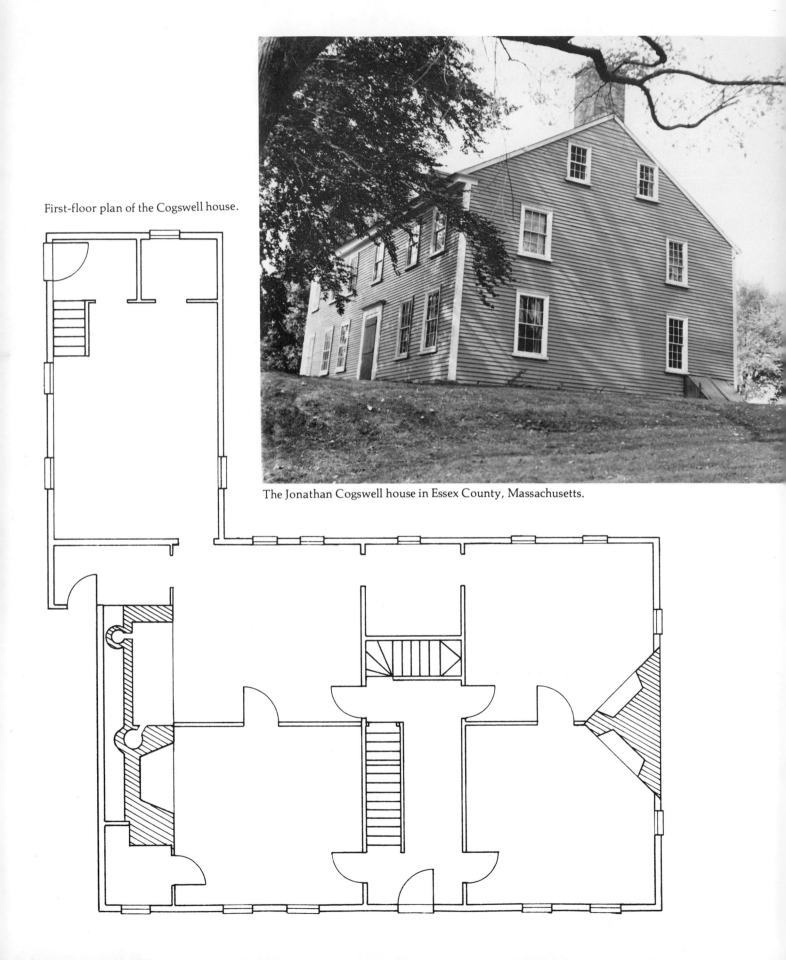

First-floor plan of the Cogswell house.

The Jonathan Cogswell house in Essex County, Massachusetts.

possessions. The rooms in his house consisted of a parlor, a parlor chamber, hall, and hall chamber, old and new kitchens with chambers, pantries, and several small rooms. This listing suggests that only half of the present house existed when Jonathan died. His farm was stocked with 18 cows, 6 yoke of oxen, 110 sheep, and 9 swine.

The contents of his house are not the typical possessions of a farmer, but it should be pointed out that Jonathan Cogswell was a wealthy farmer. Among his possessions listed were two silver tankards, valued at one hundred dollars, one silver cup, three silver porringers, and eight silver spoons. On a large dresser in his house stood thirty-four pewter plates, twelve pewter platters, three pewter basins, and many small pewter pieces. This period of time is regarded as the heyday of pewter, and it was very logical for him to have so many pieces.

Curiously, in every room there was a set of ten or twelve chairs, variously called "Carver," "cane," and "black," the total numbering seventy. And in every room but the parlor and the kitchen stood a large bed hung with curtains to keep out the cold drafts.

Cogswell owned a large number of cooking utensils, such as kettles and skillets of brass, box irons, trammels on which to hang pots, slices for lifting the pies out of ovens, and thirty-four milk pans and pots.

The writer of the Cogswell account points out that the present house is definitely not seventeenth century; however, there are a few vestiges of that era. The bricks are rather crudely made and are laid in mud instead of mortar. Each fireplace has a lug pole, and all the flues are lined with clay mixed with chopped marsh grass, as was done in earlier years in England. The size and construction of the chimney suggest that it was built in the seventeenth century and may well have been a part of William's house.

The present house is built of heavy oak timbers, but only the timbers of the basement have seventeenth-century-style chamfers, suggesting that they were formerly used in an earlier house. The roof pitch is of the eighteenth century, and the original paneling seems to be of the same era.

It is further pointed out that "the easterly end of the house was built shortly after the westerly end, (ca. 1752) as two sets of sills and girts, and a cut in the outer boarding proves."

The first-floor plan shows a central hall, and in back of the front staircase is an unusual narrow staircase, probably intended for servants who had quarters on the third floor. In back of this staircase is a small room that the present owners call a buttery.

For the most part the rooms are arranged in a conventional way, although the fireplaces are arranged strangely. *The Cogswell Family History* provides the following account:

> Mention should be made of the space between the back wall
> of the westerly chimney, and the brick-filled end of the house.
> This space reaches from the cellar to the attic, and is wide

Early-nineteenth-century Cape Cod–styled farmhouse owned by Albert B. Loring, at Norwell, Massachusetts.

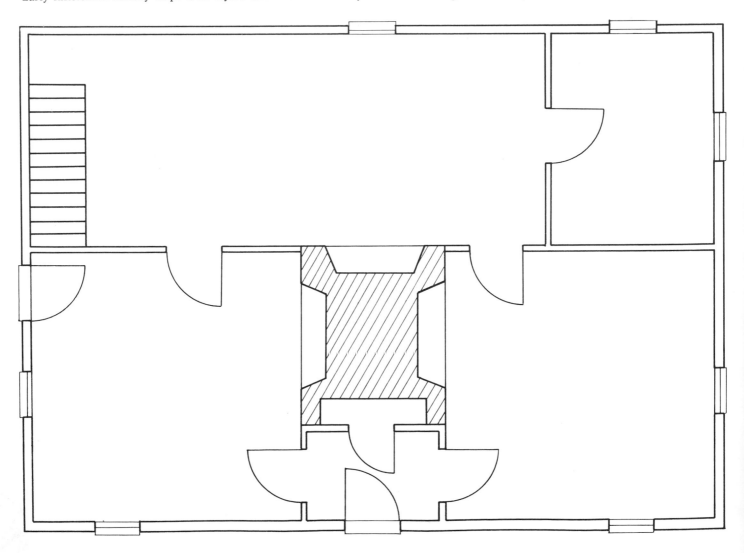

enough for a man to stand in. It is reached by a small door leading from a closet on the second floor, and was probably left to afford room for the projecting domes of the two brick ovens in the rear of the kitchen fireplace. The oven at the right we believe the oldest, as the inside is laid with clay, and it was evidently constructed before the end of the house was built, as it stands almost clear of the end studs. The left oven, which runs into the brickwork between the kitchen and the parlor fireplace, was built at a somewhat later date as the inside is laid in mortar, and the end is jammed up against the outer end of the house. . . . The domes of both ovens, however, are covered with clay mixed with marsh grass, the mixture which lines the chimney flue.

Finally, the account states that:

With the exception of a two room addition to the north-westerly side of the ell, we have made no structural changes whatever in the old house, have moved no partitions, changed no woodwork, except as noted in one room, replastered no ceilings or walls, cut no doors. As far as we can tell, the house remains the same as when it was built, and we hope and believe that it still has a long and useful life ahead.

The author visited the Cogswell house on a crisp New England October day, and it was a thrilling experience to find this masterpiece of architecture intact and in such lovely condition. It beckons one to live there and continue farming as the Cogswells did many years ago. Fortunately, someone is carrying on the traditions and chores of the farm, assisted by a few modern conveniences.

First floor plan of the Loring farmhouse.

3 Connecticut

The American farmhouse often developed and expanded in the following fashion: The original one-room house, with a fireplace and chimney in one end, was expanded by adding another room on the chimney end of the house. This new room usually housed a fireplace and flue, which became joined with and integral parts of the original fireplace and chimney. The next step was to add a second floor of two rooms, with or without fireplaces. The third step was to build a lean-to across the back of the house, with a third fireplace attached to the original chimney. This lean-to was usually divided into three rooms: a bedroom at one end, a kitchen in the middle, and a dairy room or workroom at the other end.

In contrast, the Merrill house of New Hartford, Connecticut, was built entirely as a saltbox. During the late 1720s and early 1730s, Hartford, Connecticut, was growing into a rather congested area. Abel Merrill left his home community and moved westward into Connecticut, to an area which became known as New Hartford. Although the legal name of the area remained as New Hartford, it was popularly called the "Merrill district," because so many people by that name settled there. By this time the settlers were erecting complete saltbox houses rather than building the smaller two-room cottages and gradually making additions.

In his book entitled *The Early Domestic Architecture of Connecticut*, J. Frederick Kelly writes:

> By this period a new generation had begun to take the place of the original settlers; times were rapidly becoming prosperous and general conditions much more secure. There was no longer the urgent necessity to clear land and guard against Indian attacks. Families had increased in size and wealth, and it was

26

becoming possible to devote much more attention to the physical home.

The lean-to, at first merely an addition, presently became an integral part of the construction. The additional space originally gained had become, owing to changes in the mode of living, a sheer necessity. This phase may be regarded as the fourth in the development of the house plan.

Abel Merrill was a member of this new generation described by Kelly. In the case of the Merrill house, a partial cellar was built under the house, along with a massive stone foundation, appearing to the viewer, even today, to be everlasting. For other houses in the area where there were no cellars, substantial foundation walls were built of stones. Giant hewed sills were laid on the foundations, and complete superstructures were made and fitted by tenon and mortise joinings that were usually pinned to keep them in place. Exterior walls were made of clapboards, while interior walls were of plaster.

The Merrill house did much more than meet the minimal standards for housing at that time and place. Considerable care and skill were lavished on the front door and doorway. In some ways this doorway resembles the fine examples found in Deerfield, Massachusetts.

The fireplace pictured opposite is indicative of the sophisticated interior decor. The fireplace wall is beautifully paneled, while an arched lintel spans the top of the fireplace and fluted, simulated columns flank the central panel over the fireplace. The front section of each jamb consists of one large stone, scored with demarcations to resemble an aggregate of stones laid one on top of the other. This procedure is known as coining. A similar treatment is found in the fireplace of the room on the other side of the chimney. There is also a small chamber for smoking meat adjoining this other fireplace. Most noteworthy is the fact that the panel display is so completely original.

The floor plan of the Merrill house provides for front and rear staircases to the second floor. Quarters for servants occupied the third floor, and entry was by way of the front stairs. The original floors are in fairly good condition and, with a little care, they will serve for another century or two.

The Merrills were originally engaged in the lumber business until their land and that of others nearby was cleared, after which they became farmers. Their farm originally consisted of 144 acres, about 50 of which are suitable for farming today. The present owners are Mr. and Mrs. Roy Robbins.

Another significant farmhouse in the New England area is the home of Mr. and Mrs. Sperry Morway, located in Glastonbury, Connecticut. The rear section is the oldest part of this house, having been built in 1687. Originally, it too consisted of only two rooms, with a chimney between and a fireplace in each room. Under the fireplaces and hearths are gigantic stone piers, which support the masonry construction above. This huge mass of masonry remains intact today and occupies much of the space in the cellar. The remaining cellar area is used for dry storage.

End view of the Abel Merrill saltbox house, now owned by Mr. and Mrs. Roy Robbins. Located near New Hartford, Connecticut.

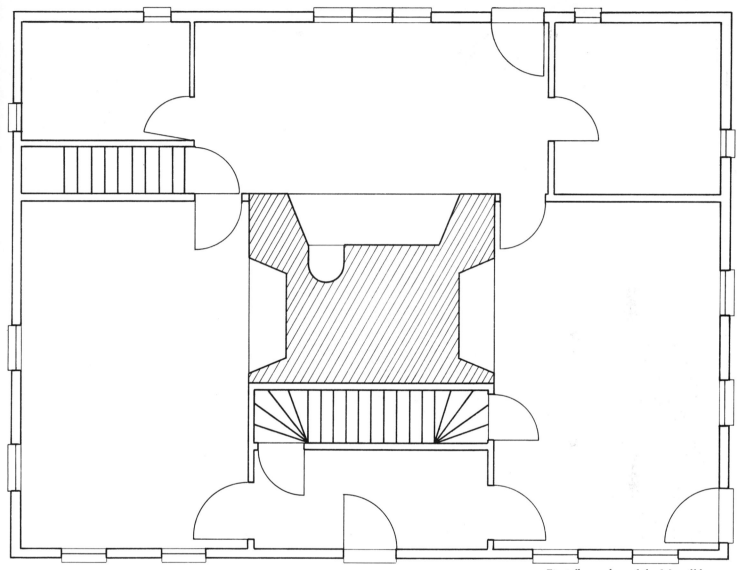

First-floor plan of the Merrill house.

Fireplace in the Merrill house.

The front, or second part, of the house was added in 1716. On the first floor, there are two fireplaces with attractive panels above them and to each side. The windows, which extend to the rather low ceiling, are particularly interesting because of their "Indian shutters." These slide in grooves above the chair rails and in moldings at the ceiling level. The shutters are beautifully paneled and can be positioned to cover the windows at night, to shut out the cold, and to protect the inhabitants from marauding Indians. Similar shutters exist in other houses in this area. On the south side of the house are a scullery and borning room.

The front door is a double one, secured only by slipping a bar of wood into iron hoops near the middle of the door. The most interesting door on the first floor is located on a side wall near the front. This door was known as the coffin door, because its location allowed the easy removal of a coffin from the interior of the house. Many front halls and front doors were built very narrow in these early farmhouses, and coffin doors are found with unexpected frequency.

Another unusual feature of the Morway house is its gambrel roof, which not only covers the front and back sections but also extends around the corners of the two sections. Gambrel roofs were invented in Europe when houses were taxed according to their number of floors. A room under a roof was considered an attic; thus a house with a gambrel roof had only one taxable floor. The dormers in this gambrel roof are known as pierced dormers. Adjoining a second-floor fireplace is a smoke oven for the curing of meat.

The farm, of which this house was the focal point, was a prosperous undertaking for many years. Sections of it were laid out for intensive farming, other areas for meadowland, and a portion was preserved as a wooded section to supply local farmers with firewood and other wood products. Now it is a townhouse with only memories of its farming days.

Another interesting farmhouse is a Victorian house that was built in 1861 and is located in Kensington, Connecticut. It is presently owned and occupied by Mr. and Mrs. Frank Kimball. One would expect its floor plan to be quite different from those previously examined. In some ways, however, it is not all that different, since many Georgian features have been incorporated. It is evident, however, that certain rooms serve certain functions, regardless of how they are arranged within.

There is a Victorian porch at the front door, and the cornice and frieze are ornamented in traditional Victorian manner. The small size of the porch suggests that it served as a protection for callers as they waited entry into the house and was not geared for a family rocking-chair brigade. There is a smaller porch at one end of the house, which probably was used by less formal callers. And, of course, there is a door at the back of the house that leads to the backyard and the barn. A small protective roof was installed over this door in modern times.

Inside the front door is a graceful hall with a curving stair that leads to the second floor. A door at the rear opens into the combination kitchen and dining room. To the left of the hall is a parlor and a first-floor bedroom. Across the back of these two rooms and the hall is the kitchen–dining room, a pleasant and spacious room which retains its original fireplace.

Behind the kitchen-dining room are two rooms: One possibly served as a storage area, while the other was obviously a work kitchen. Part of the storage room is now being utilized as a bathroom. In the work kitchen there is an old-fashioned bake oven, but it is no longer used. It is in perfect condition and could be readied for baking at a few minutes' notice.

The exterior of the house is typical of those built in 1861. For example, there is a very broad overhang at the cornice that presumably protected the outer walls from the deteriorating effects of hostile weather. Beneath the cornice is a frieze that is intercepted by very short attic windows. A tower on the roof is decorative but of doubtful importance. Both the interior and exterior of this house have been kept in shipshape condition.

The owner refers to his farm as a "one-horse" farm, because it originally consisted of only thirteen acres, along with a barn that was proportionate to the size of the farm. In addition, a two-horse team could not have entered the main barn floor, nor could it have survived on the contents of the storage mows.

The Victorian farmhouse is an outstanding example of many that still survive throughout the countryside.

4 Vermont

The farmhouse of Prof. and Mrs. Alexander Luce, located in Windsor County, near Springfield, Vermont, was built in 1790. The house was built by a man named Fletcher, who had eight sons and one daughter. One son, Frink, lived in the house for eighty-two years. Another son, Deal Fletcher, was an artist of considerable ability, who painted local landscapes and portraits. Lyman Fletcher was a fiddler and played for dances in the area. In 1885 George Tanner bought the farm from Frink Fletcher's widow and two sons. Following Mr. Tanner's ownership of nearly fifty years, the house was occupied by a succession of families, until the present owners, the Luces, bought the farm in 1941.

This sturdy house is forty-four feet by thirty-five feet, and it is built on a rocky ledge with the bases of the two chimneys measuring four feet square. The granite for the foundation is thought to have come from Scrabble Quarry nearby. Like many farmhouses in this survey, this one faces south, so that as many windows as possible can catch the winter sunshine.

The house is a five-bay, two-chimney type. The frame is connected with mortise and tenon joints, held securely in place by wooden pins. The interior walls are of plank on which laths are nailed and the walls plastered. The original wide floorboards remain in all rooms except the kitchen. The original small panes of glass in the windows were replaced by larger ones when they became available; however, the Luces restored the small panes.

The floor plan is a modified Georgian style with the center hall terminating in the kitchen, instead of running continuously from the front door to the back door. This plan made a sizable amount of space available for the kitchen which otherwise would have been wasted on the center hall. There are four fireplaces on each floor, including two cooking fireplaces on the first

Farmhouse and barn of Prof. and Mrs. Alexander Luce, near Springfield, Vermont. Photo by Courtney Fisher. Courtesy of Vermont Division of Historic Sites.

First-floor plan of the Luce farmhouse.

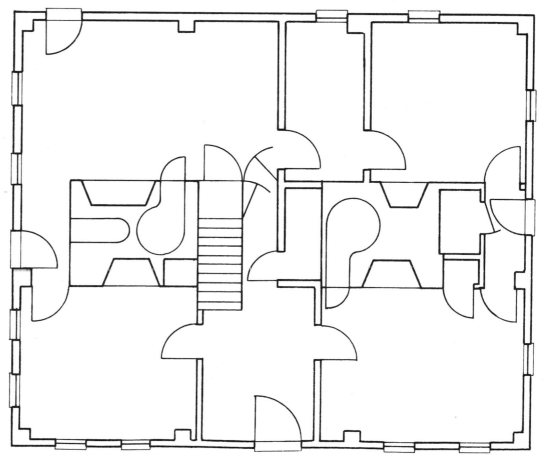

The Enos farmhouse built ca. 1790 in the vicinity of Lyme, Grafton County, New Hampshire. This house is a typical example of a New England rural building, a continuous farm structure consisting of a house, sheds, and barns. Photo reproduction from the Library of Congress Collection. Courtesy of the Historic American Buildings Survey.

Fall scene at Howe Farms in Turnbridge, Vermont. Courtesy of the Agency of Development and Community Affairs.

floor. These were necessary because the house originally was occupied by two married brothers. Each had a separate entry to the cellar, although both used the same set of stairs. In addition, each end of the house had its own doorway. Each chimney has four flues, and the west chimney has a smoke chamber for smoking meat. This chamber was more practical than operating a smokehouse in the backyard.

A bit of romance is related in Mrs. Luce's account of a tree on the property, which was recorded in *The Historical Houses of Springfield, Vermont:*

> In the front yard is a 60-year-old arbor vitae, or white cedar tree. It was planted in 1906, the year in which Mr. Tanner's daughter, Viola, was married in the southwest parlor. She and her husband, Fred Parker, went to Maine on their honeymoon and brought the tree home in their suitcase and planted it in the doorway of the bride's old home, as was a charming custom, hence its designation as a Bridal or Marriage Tree. Anniversary and wedding receptions have been held in its shade by the present owners, and the Parkers were photographed under the tree on their 50th anniversary.

In its day the Luce farm was very productive. Among its crops were buckwheat, popcorn, field corn, currants, raspberries, blackberries, gooseberries, apples, pears, plums, quinces, and grapes. Quantities of maple sugar and syrup were shipped to many distant points. The pigs provided vast amounts of ham and bacon, and the chickens produced more eggs than were needed for home use. There were horses to till the land and to haul the produce to its destination.

Although several of the sheds were lost to heavy snowstorms, two large cow barns, a horse barn, a milk house, and attached woodshed still remain. Early photographs of the site portray a typical New England farmhouse with a continuous string of attached buildings trailing in the rear, so that all areas could be reached without battling the weather. Today, a fine old home survives which with care and affection will serve for many more years.

Part II
THE MIDDLE STATES

5 The Hudson River Valley

The survey of farmhouses now turns to one of the unique regions in America, namely, the Hudson River Valley. This area was not entirely an island of Dutch culture, as many are apt to think of it. Thomas Wertenbaker points out in *The Founding of American Civilization, the Middle Colonies* that when the English took over the region in 1664 there were only about eight thousand Dutch living there. The records of the Dutch Reformed Church in New Amsterdam from 1639 to 1659 show that only 59 percent of the inhabitants were Dutch, the balance being composed of French, Flemings, Walloons, and English.

There were several reasons why Manhattan and the Hudson River Valley did not fill up rapidly with Dutch colonists. At the time of colonization, the Dutch, having won their war with Spain, were free to nurture their economy with amazing skill and ingenuity. They had gained precious land space by building dikes to exclude the sea. This gave them more living space. Shipbuilding prospered before the end of the sixteenth century, when they were reported to have been building two thousand ships a year. In 1634 the Dutch fleet consisted of approximately thirty-five thousand vessels. They could be found in the ports of Spain, France, Italy, Russia, Sweden, and the British Isles. In addition to their extensive foreign trade, a fine network of canals and rivers at home offered cheap and efficient transportation.

In 1621 the Dutch West India Company was organized with the authority to maintain and govern colonies. Unfortunately for the welfare of future colonies, the goals of this enterprise were to show a profit for the investors and to promote the prestige of the homeland. Its affairs were controlled by a board of directors whose major interest was in obtaining high dividends for the company. One of their notable achievements was the capture of a Spanish "Silver Fleet" valued at twenty million florins.

Responsibility for the settlement of the Hudson Valley was given to this organization. Since a new settlement, for obvious reasons, did not show an immediate profit, support for it was lukewarm. There was the prospect of a flourishing fur trade with the Indians in the hinterland, for which skilled craftsmen at home produced desirable objects for barter, such as guns, knives, blankets, clothes, and probably hard liquor. The projected lumber industry was handicapped by high labor costs and the expense of shipping from great distances rather than from nearby countries on the Baltic. The convenience of the river kept the docks of New Amsterdam bustling with activity, but clearing the land and growing crops returned low income, and it developed at a much slower pace.

An attempt was made to encourage activity in the West India Company by granting large tracts of land to stockholders. The intent was to re-create a feudal colony in America, complete with a lord of the manor and many peasant farmers. This scheme was unsuccessful, since the vassals learned that land was cheap and plentiful in New Jersey and Pennsylvania and therefore they would not be induced to live as peons.

The area around Manhattan, Long Island, and Staten Island did present opportunities for the free farmer. There he could clear land, plant and harvest crops, and take them to market in Manhattan. Back from the Hudson lay other rich plots of land which individual farmers soon acquired. They raised grain in their fields, fed and butchered cattle, and exchanged butter, cheese, and vegetables for beautiful and useful articles from abroad. The farmers prospered, but it was the merchants who profited most and ruled the colony. They furnished their homes with textiles, as well as objects of silver, pewter, and copper. The farmer could afford very few of these luxuries.

Despite the fact that much of the population in the Valley was not Dutch in origin, the popular image of the region is that it was filled with Dutch houses and barns, perhaps because they were so different from others, particularly the English. An outstanding study, *Dutch Houses of the Hudson Valley before 1776*, was written in 1929 by Helen Wilkinson Reynolds. At that time there was an appalling deterioration in the farmhouses of the Valley; many were in shambles, only a few were updated in style and accommodations, and virtually none survived in their original indoor or outdoor pattern.

Reynolds takes us back to the very beginning, when the land was cleared, the first crops were planted, and the first houses were built. While researching her book, Reynolds discovered that the earliest Dutch farmhouses were actually cellar-houses. According to one report made by Cornelius Van Tienhoven in 1650, who was then secretary of New Amsterdam, the families dug a hole in the ground six or seven feet deep, and as long and broad as needed. They laid a floor with planks, covered the walls with bark, and made the roof of spars that were then covered with bark and sod. Partitions were made according to the demands of the family. Van Tienhoven recommended that colonists arrive in March or April, in order that they have the summer before them to dig their cellars and plant their crops.

The farmer in the Valley, as in many other regions, planted corn and beans in his fields. In his garden he grew parsnips, carrots, and cabbages; all grew well in the virgin soil. In the summer pigs grazed in nearby woods on acorns. In the fall they were fed corn to fatten them for butchering. In the second year the farmer could look forward to the purchase of cattle, which he sheltered in his Dutch barn.

The first Dutch farmhouses that were built above the ground were constructed either of logs or boards, usually of one room with a loft overhead. It is interesting to note how similar the first houses were, no matter in which geographical areas of the New World they were built. The most primitive type had a smoke hole in the roof; later ones had a wooden chimney.

Some of the first permanent farmhouses were built substantially of stone. One standing intact as it was built in 1663 is the first Bronck house at Coxsackie. By the terms of his patent from the Dutch government, Pieter Bronck was required to build a house on his land within a period of two years.

The first house built on his 325 acres has a sharply pitched straight roof, giving adequate "head room" on the second floor. In one gable and on the first floor are two large windows with nine panes over nine. On the second floor there are casement windows, above which are two portholes presumably for using firearms. A chimney is located in the west wall, wide boards compose the floor, and the bull's-eye windows are thought to be original.

The date 1685 is cut into the upper beam of a stone in the first addition that was made to the house. The doorway in the addition has a door with a transom, probably once filled with bull's-eye panes, and a charming stoop with a baluster but no supporting posts for the roof. The doorway is flanked on one side by a single casement, on the other side by two double-casement windows.

A covered passageway connects the original stone house with a large brick structure, built in 1738. Presumably this was also built to accommodate family expansion. The only data available about it is that it "became the prosperous county seat of Leonard Bronck, Greene County's first judge of the court of Common Pleas, 1800–1810."

Before pursuing the subject of farmhouse architecture in the Hudson Valley any further, it should be noted that there was a distinct variance between the farmhouses of the Netherlands and those of the New World. Dutch farmhouses, like those in Bavaria, often are part of a large structure that includes both house and barn. In Pennsylvania it is possible that at least one such structure was built, but no architectural historians have mentioned the presence of any in the Hudson Valley. The reason why this traditional

The first Pieter Bronck house in Coxsackie, New York, built in 1663.

44

The second Bronck house built in 1685.

The third Bronck house built in 1738.

and practical structure was never adopted in America is difficult to understand. Both the Dutch and the Germans clung to many aspects of their homeland culture in the New World. The Dutch continued to build jambless fireplaces, for example, even though they were obviously not as safe or functional as the enclosed English type. They hung a chimney cloth on the edge of the hood over the fireplace, and used traditional tiles on the back wall. However, although they built uniquely Dutch houses and barns, the two buildings were never combined.

A common pattern evolved in the first permanent houses in the Hudson Valley. Generally speaking, the earliest farmhouses were built of stone, later ones of brick. This choice of materials can be traced back to the Netherlands where the scarcity of wood dictated that houses be built of masonry materials. In America, although wood was plentiful, the lasting value of stone probably outweighed the benefits of the easier construction of a house of wood. The houses were usually one and a half stories high, with a straight slanting roof of thatch in the rural areas, of tiles later in the towns. The danger of fires caused by sparks from the chimney tipped the scales toward tiles as soon as they were available. However, I haven't ever found or read about a single house in the Valley that has retained a roof of tile. An interesting feature of these houses is the door, separated horizontally into two halves, each opening independently, and known as Dutch doors.

The first house visited by the author in the Hudson Valley is located near Ghent, New York, and owned by Mrs. Teresa Scafero.

The owner of this house has no documented information about its age. The presence of a cellar together with its large size suggest that it was built very late in the seventeenth century or early in the eighteenth. It seems unique to the area in which it is located.

Stone farmhouse near Ghent, New York, owned and occupied by Mrs. Teresa Scafero. The ridgepole of this house is on the short axis.

First-floor plan of Scafero house.

46

This structure may have contained two rooms at one time, although at present it consists of one large room approximately twenty-two feet by thirty feet. Off-center in one end wall is a fireplace, and next to it is a closet with a very small window. The window appears to be original, the enclosure is not. At the opposite end is a substantial staircase that leads to the second floor. Its location and construction suggests that it is the original staircase. One window with nine panes over nine is probably not original to the house; however, the drawing of the Jan Martense Schenck house (1675) shows a similar arrangement of lights. Like many early houses, this one abuts against a later addition, the only alteration being the substitution of a door for a window.

Attention is now directed to the Jan Martense Schenck house, originally located in the Brooklyn area on an offshore island. Much of the information about this house has been taken from a booklet written by Marvin D. Schwartz, a curator of the Brooklyn Museum, where the house is now located. The house was identified as a farmhouse in a 1796 assessment roll which described it as being thirty-one by twenty-two feet, with a barn forty-two by forty-four feet, and a mill twenty-eight by twenty-eight feet. It has undergone many alterations from the time it was built in 1675 until it was dismantled in 1952.

The fact that the house was built of wood distinguishes it from most farmhouses built in the Valley, although there were counterparts of it in the region. The earliest view known of New Amsterdam, published in 1651, pictures a group of clapboard houses, some having vertical boarding instead of the horizontal type that is found on the Schenck house.

As the house was carefully dismantled, the major mode of construction could be ascertained, largely through the work on timbers and the way they were assembled. The original framework was carefully joined with mortise and tenon joints, the mating pieces being identified by identical Roman numerals cut upon them.

It was found that the first floor consisted of two rooms of about equal size, with fireplaces back to back in the middle of the partition. Presumably these were Dutch-type fireplaces without jambs as found on English fireplaces. There are few openings in the outer walls of the house. On the east wall a door and a window duplicated similar openings on the south wall. Openings were kept at a minimum for protection against the cold and intruders. Two bed boxes were built on the inside against the blank north wall, and on the outside along the west wall a roof extended as a meager protection for farm animals. There was a winding stair in one corner against a partition wall. It is believed that in the nineteenth century the attic was divided into bed and storage rooms.

Considerable research went into determining the colors of paint used on the house. The original clapboards had only one coat of paint which proved to have been dark gray. A sand color was used on the window frames, and the shutters were painted green. These colors also were used on contemporary structures in the Netherlands.

Rendering of the Jan Martense Schenck house as it appeared in 1675. Executed by Ian Smith, 1963. Courtesy of the Brooklyn Museum.

View of the timbers in the reconstructed Jan Martense Schenck house. Two parts are marked. Courtesy of the Brooklyn Museum.

North room showing a bed box in the Jan Martense Schenck house reconstructed in the Brooklyn Museum. Courtesy of the Brooklyn Museum.

South room of the Jan Martense Schenck house showing fireplace with appropriate fittings.
Courtesy of the Brooklyn Museum.

No early inventory of the furnishings has survived, so it was necessary to choose them by hypothesis. One room was without bed boxes and this obviously was the kitchen, the center of interest being the Dutch fireplace with its hood and chimney cloth. A hood is dropped down about eighteen inches from the ceiling, forming a rectangular funnel to direct the smoke into the chimney. There are no jambs on either side of the fireplaces. A rack molding decorates the bottom edge of the hood, an area where the Dutch displayed their fine china and metalware. A fireback stands on the hearth floor against the back wall of the fireplace to protect it from continued crumbling as a result of the heat. The iron andirons have spit hooks, and a trammel is hooked on a lug pole located in the throat of the chimney. There is no crane. The forepart of the hearth is a very large stone, its size obviously related to safety requirements.

The floor is not covered but polished to a fine texture by constant scrubbing with sand. The walls are plastered; however, there is no plaster on the ceiling between the beams. The knee braces give the beams support and add a decorative touch to the architecture of the room.

The kitchen is sparsely furnished, as it probably was originally, with a large and a small table, a cupboard and a chest, and several ladder-back chairs. A few decorative items are hung on the wall.

The bedroom-parlor is also sparsely furnished. Between the bed boxes stands a large kas, obviously a storage place for clothing and bed linens. Many similar objects have been reported to have come from the Hudson Valley. The upholstery on the chairs seems to have been overdone a bit, but it is consistent with the rich table cover. The floor and walls are treated in a way similar to those in the kitchen.

This survey of seventeenth-century farmhouses in the Hudson Valley shows that there was a unique development there largely under Dutch influence. However, on a fringe of the Valley, in Rockland County, New York, and Bergen County, New Jersey, a different breed of houses is found, which defied identification for some time. Thomas Wertenbaker in his *The Founding of American Civilization, The Middle Colonies* writes:

> Entirely unlike the houses of the Albany region are the so-called Dutch farmhouses of southern New York and northeastern New Jersey. One finds today, lost in the maze of suburban Brooklyn, or overlooking the Hackensack, or tucked away in some little valley of Rockland County, these charming relics of the time of Rip Van Winkle and Ichabod Crane.

For many years the European origin of these houses with so-called flying gutters was not known. Wertenbaker points out that the search for the origin of these houses focused in the area of the low countries called Flanders: "This leads us directly to the maritime sections of Flanders, the region embracing the extreme northern tip of France, western Belgium, and parts of Zeeland in Holland."

The heavy hand of war, poverty, and political oppression forced the Flemings to leave their homeland. Many fled to the Netherlands, where if they were craftsmen, they found a workbench or loom where they could continue with their trade. But the farmer could not buy land in the Netherlands. It was a precious commodity, and no Dutchman would sell his plot to a foreigner. With nothing but trouble behind them, many set sail for America. When they got there, they sought land, and it was easily available in the areas described. There the farmer built a home of native red sandstone, one and one half stories high, further distinguished by a rise of the roof at the cornice, some being squared underneath, others having a concave shape. The distance which this roof projected varied in each house, some extending so far as to virtually form a porch to which posts were added. The proposed origin of this flying gutter was to protect the poor mortar used in houses in Europe, but the well-built stone houses with lime mortar in America did not need such protection. The obvious reason for its persistence was the pleasure derived from a foreign, yet familiar architectural heritage lending variety and style to one area of the New World.

The farmhouses in Rockland County that are to be examined were built in the eighteenth century. The first to come under scrutiny is the Blauvelt-Secor house. This relatively small farmhouse, being only twenty-two by thirty-three feet, is an I-shaped structure having no appendage on the rear. The photograph of it shows a chimney on the near end, but there is also one on the far end, both connected to a fireplace on the first floor. Most importantly, the view also shows the flying gutter, which identifies the house as Dutch-Flemish. The framing under the gutter in this house is square, the framing under the flying gutter of the next house is concave.

On the first floor there are two rooms about equal in size, divided by a very narrow steep staircase which leads to the second floor. The stairway to the cellar is equally steep and narrow. These two rooms served the traditional functions. One was a kitchen that also served as a dining room, an all-purpose room of the house. The cooking and eating was done there, as well as baking, the oven being built against an outer wall, but with access from within the house. The other room was a parlor, containing at least one bed and furnishings with which to entertain guests. Neighbors were probably welcomed in the kitchen, while the minister and local dignitaries were entertained in the parlor.

The traditional precaution of constructing only a few openings in the house was also followed. On the first floor, there are only two windows in the back wall, matching two in the front of the house. There is one in each end wall, one of them being very small. The outstanding feature of the openings, however, is the presence of two very attractive front doors. The reason for having two front doors on houses in this area is said to be that originally the farmers built small stone houses with one front door. When space was needed for a married child, a house was expanded by building a stone addition. Since two families were involved, and it was very difficult to

End view of the Blauvelt-Secor house in Rockland County, New York. Courtesy of Misses Eleanor Fitch and Gladys Weber.

First-floor plan of Blauvelt-Secor house.

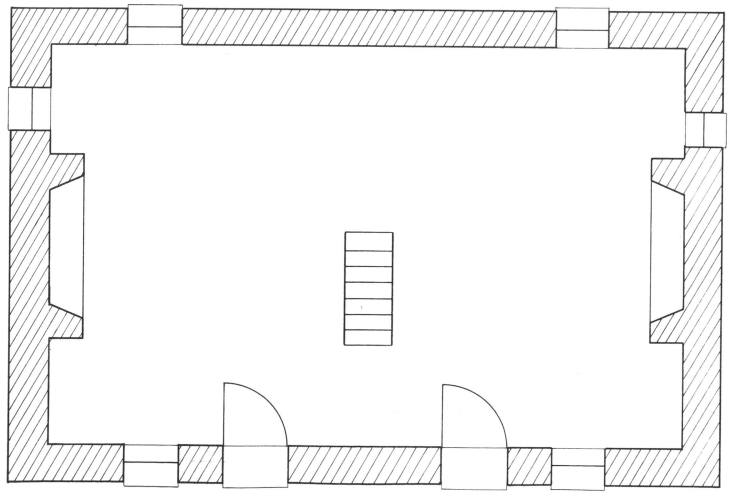

cut a doorway through the first stone house, the two-door facade became quite common. The procedure proved to be so popular that, when a large house was built from scratch, often two doors were installed. Although the Blauvelt-Secor house is not a large one, it has two front doors. It might also be pointed out that the doors in this house are divided horizontally. This practice was followed so that fresh air could be brought into the rooms, but the occasional fowl from the barnyard could be kept out. The doors are nicely paneled, so that one might say that two doors are more attractive than one.

The next house in Rockland County (located at Spring Valley) to be considered is much larger than the Blauvelt-Secor house, this one being approximately thirty feet wide and forty feet long. In the tradition of Dutch-Flemish house construction of the eighteenth century, the original part of this house consisted of only one room, built in 1735. When the second and sizable part was built in 1760, the builder fell under the spell of Georgian architecture, and the house was expanded to have a central hall, with two rooms on each side of the first floor.

Three sides of the house were built of cut stones, the rear wall being constructed of fieldstones. The reason for this procedure is not apparent—perhaps for variety. However, there certainly was little economy in the procedure. The roof is a Dutch gambrel type with a flying gutter, a roof

The Dutch-Flemish Smith house ca. 1735 and ca. 1760 located at Spring Valley in Rockland County.

style that is considered to be one of the most attractive used in America. The gable ends of the second floor are covered with shingles. The rooms are approximately fifteen feet square, and all four on the first floor have fireplaces built against an outer wall. The presence of only two chimneys above the roof line can be explained by the fact that the four flues converge in pairs under the roof.

The outside cellar door is a typical feature of farmhouses and probably leads to a partial cellar beneath the house.

The Jacob Blauvelt house in Rockland County is also a very good example of Dutch-Flemish architecture. It has a typical gambrel roof with flying gutters, as can be clearly observed in the photograph of the end wall of the house. The main house and the appendages are all built of brick on the first floor and of clapboard on the second floor. The contrasting shutters of white, red, and green make a very colorful and pleasing arrangement.

Like many houses that have been discussed in this survey, the Blauvelt house was built in two parts. The small kitchen wing was built between 1780 and 1790; the rest of the house was built in 1834. Attached to the kitchen wing is a summer kitchen, which was probably built when the house was enlarged.

The main block of the house has a very pleasant, but unorthodox arrangement of rooms. One enters a foyer inside the front door, which gives access to the three rooms of the main block and to the kitchen as well. On the first floor of the main house are two parallel rooms, running lengthwise. There are fireplaces in each room as indicated by the chimneys. One of these rooms is furnished like a parlor, the other a bedroom. Crosswise, at the end of these rooms is a foyer and another small room, now furnished as a bedroom. Originally, this was more than likely a sewing room or a study, as there are several bedrooms on the second floor. The one large bedroom on the first floor is not unusual, since many farmhouses have been found with a similar arrangement. This house is now owned by the Rockland County Historical Society.

The last house in this survey of the Rockland County area is a fine old farmhouse that is built of clapboard, one and a half stories high. The oldest section is the right wing including the door and two windows, with a width of twenty-two feet. Originally, there were two rooms on the first floor, the front one being obviously the kitchen, for the fireplace is located there, and there was a beehive bake oven against the masonry rear wall of the fireplace. This was removed before the present owner acquired the house in 1928. The back room has now been divided into two rooms. About 1860 the second part of the house was built, it being a duplicate of the first part. An ample hall was provided between the two parts with a staircase that leads to the second floor.

In one way this was a unique farmhouse, for it was located in the center of one of the first large apple orchards in the state of New York. It continues to

The Jacob Blauvelt house, now owned by the Rockland County Historical Society.

First-floor plan of the Jacob Blauvelt house.

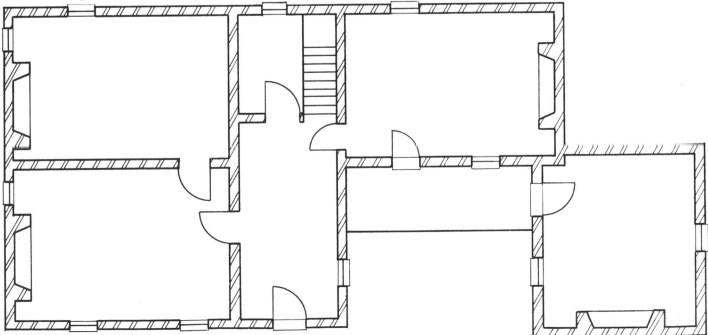

End view of the Jacob Blauvelt house.

be surrounded with apple trees. The charming old photograph of the house has been provided by the present owner, J. Irwin Perine.

Back along the river, there are three farmhouses of interest, one of the eighteenth century and two of the nineteenth century. In each case all evidence of the original Dutch influence has disappeared.

The house of the eighteenth century is a fine stone house, built in 1740 near Ghent by Johannes Hogeboom. This house is an example of Georgian architecture, with only a little variance. It is beautifully situated on a hill where the farmer could conveniently view his outbuildings and fields. Possibly the most interesting facet of the house is the outer two-part wall that is two and a half feet thick, with a six-inch air space between the two walls. A smaller air space is known in a wall of another house. This feature was presumably to prevent water leakage through a stone wall into the inner wall of the house.

The J. Irwin Perine house near Spring Valley, New York. Photograph courtesy of J. Irwin Perine.

First-floor plan of the Hogeboom house.

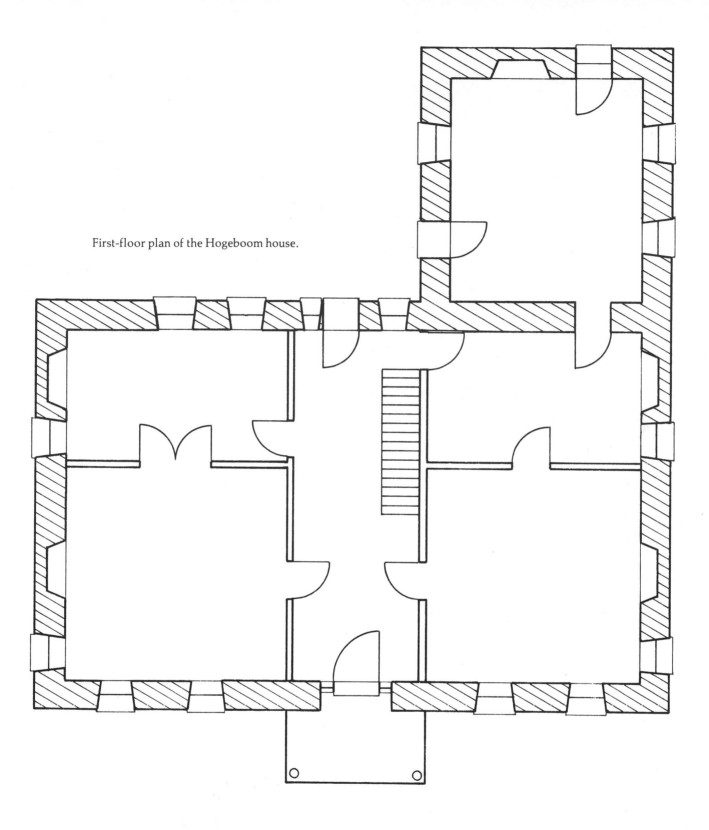

The Johannes Hogeboom house, ca. 1740, is now the residence of Mr. and Mrs. James L. Salerno, at Ghent, New York. It is called Broad Stairs because of the unusual width of the halls and stairs.

A farmhouse that is an example of rural Greek Revival architecture is now the residence of Mr. and Mrs. Robert C. Kipp, at Claverack, New York.

60

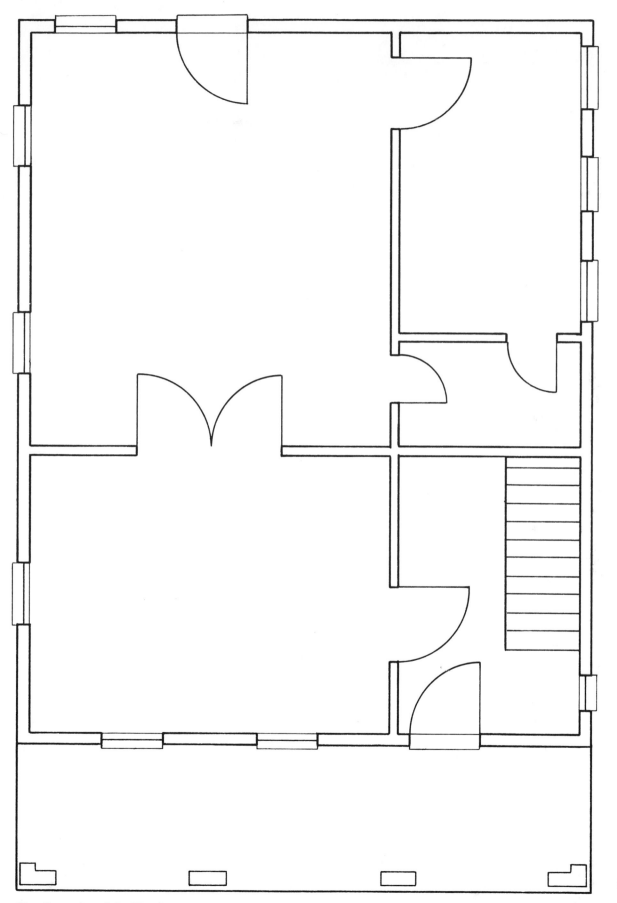

First-floor plan of the Kipp house.

The Victorian farmhouse on the L. K. Keil farmstead at Catskill.

Late-eighteenth-century Dutch farmhouse near Pine Plains in Dutchess County, New York. The porch, a second main room, and the second-story rooms were added later to the original one room. It is thought that the dormers, which are typical of this style of house, are missing because of later reconstruction to the roof. Courtesy of Donn and Anne Christine Potter.

The facade of the house is perfectly balanced in the Georgian tradition, although the hall is twelve feet wide and the two rear rooms on the first floor are smaller than the front rooms. This house has had a number of changes over the years, but the thick wall and the size of the two rear rooms have not been substantially altered.

Another charming farmhouse is an example of rural Greek Revival architecture, built about 1840. It is small, about twenty-four feet wide and thirty feet deep.

The first-floor plan is particularly interesting. Inside the front door there is a hall with a stairway straight ahead, leading to the second floor. To the left of the hall is a parlor about fifteen by sixteen feet in size. Through a typical double door, one enters the back room, presumably a combination kitchen and dining area. However, there is a wing in the back that may have served as a kitchen from the very start. To the right of the dining area and in back of the hall, there is a bedroom. There are no fireplaces in any of the rooms. The chimney seen in the photograph belongs to a modern furnace that is located in the cellar.

The most interesting feature of this house is the pediment and the pillars on and above the front porch. The corner ones are right angles, with grillwork in the panels; the other two are flat with similar panels. This farmhouse looks like a little temple in the New York countryside, although it is part of a 100-acre working farm today, the home of Mr. and Mrs. Robert C. Kipp.

Another fine example of a farmhouse in the Hudson River Valley is the Keil farmhouse located in Catskill. The house is about a hundred years old, according to the owner, and it is completely in the Victorian style, the outer walls being of solid brick construction as are also the partitions between the rooms. The projecting roof with a frieze beneath is a perfect setting for the large brackets that appear to be supporting the roof. The bay windows and the porch roof both carry the same arrangement as was used on the main roof. Under the cornice frieze is a sawtooth arrangement of bricks that is particularly attractive. The balusters of the front porch are obviously the product of a band saw, a machine that was often used in the woodwork of Victorian houses. The roof brackets were also fashioned with a band saw.

The basement door leads to a summer kitchen, in back of which is a cold cellar for food storage. The converging spouts are designed to collect rainwater for a cistern. Cistern water was used for washing and other household needs, but not for drinking. There is a springhouse nearby, which is equipped with a pump to provide running water throughout the house. There are a number of bathrooms which seem to have been installed when the house was built.

There never was a fireplace in the house. By the time this house was built, stoves were readily available.

6 The Delaware Valley

In the seventeenth century, the area of the Delaware Valley became a true melting pot with a blending of immigrants from Sweden, Finland, Germany, Switzerland, and England. The first settlement was made near Wilmington, Delaware, in 1638 by the Dutch West India Company, under the aegis of Sweden, which hired Peter Minuit (formerly governor of New Amsterdam) to found the colony there. He went ashore at the confluence of the Christina and Delaware rivers. The purpose of the colony was to create a base for trade with the Delaware and Susquehannock Indians.

Although no Swedish log cabins of the seventeenth century have survived, a reasonably good description can be obtained from observers who remember them. Several of these men have commented on the unusual location of the fireplace. Farming and trading were the earliest occupations of the Swedish settlers, and is noted by Amandus Johnson in *The Swedes on The Delaware, 1638–1664*, that:

> tobacco raising was discontinued after 1646, as it proved unprofitable. Grain and Indian corn were now the staple products, and New Sweden had become an agricultural rather than a commercial colony, due to lack of support from the mother country and the nature and inclination of the settlers.
>
> It was a remarkably beautiful (New Sweden) country with all the glories a person could wish for on earth, and a pity and regret that it was not occupied by true Christians. It was adorned with all the fruit bearing trees. The soil was suitable

for planting and sowing, and if her Majesty would but make a serious beginning, the colony would soon be a desirable place to live in.

Printz was anxious to make use of this "suitable soil" and many of the advantages found there, and it is probable that land was allotted to some of the colonists as early as March. New settlements were made at Finland, Upland (Chester), Teqirassey, Tinicum, and Providence Island (within present Philadelphia), and here freemen labored to found new homes surrounded by fertile fields.

The choice of logs as a construction material for the early farmhouses of the colonists of New Sweden was a matter of tradition and expediency. The fields were cleared of trees, which were then trimmed and laid aside in a manner that made them available for building houses. The bottom log on the four sides of the house (called *sills* in other construction) was laid on large stones, with each succeeding log notched in the adjoining one to keep the corners from separating. Openings were cut into the enclosure after it was entirely built. These usually consisted of a door—often very low by modern standards—and one window on each side. Safety was ensured by the installation of bars, and the cold was kept out by a covering of greased paper or thin skins. A primitive type of shutter was made with vertical boarding held in place by two crosswise battens. There were no cellars under the first cabins, but above the one-room apartments lofts were built for storage and as sleeping quarters for children. The roof was covered with thatch or long split shingles and held in place by heavy logs. The entire structure was built only with axes, a large one for heavy cutting and a small hand ax to notch joints for the corners. The floor at first consisted only of bare ground. Later, this was covered with split logs called puncheons.

Not only was the log house unique to this area in the seventeenth century, but its corner fireplace was an uncommon appendage at that time. First, the inner walls of the corner were covered with mud or stones to the roof line. Next, a wall was placed diagonally across the corner. The fireplace was then complete and functional, with the addition of a chimney above the roof line. This traditional plan of building log houses with corner fireplaces was probably continued for several generations, but at a later time the fireplace was relocated into an end wall. In *The Log Cabin in America*, C. A. Westlager describes a log house standing between Wilmington and Dover, Delaware, that was built of round logs (an early feature), with its chimney made of brick and set on a foundation of stones in one of the gable ends:

Although the corner fireplace and the chimney are characteristic of ancient Swedish crafts and culture, this does not mean that all builders adhered to this trait, because some of the log residences of New Sweden were built with chimneys in the gable ends, and the stick-and-mud chimney was also built when necessity demanded it.

Swedish-style log house with fireplace in the corner, near Darby, Pennsylvania. The house is no longer standing. Courtesy of the Historic American Buildings Survey.

It has been suggested that the Germans introduced the one-room cabin with its fireplace in the gable end, having used it in their homeland. Others may have found the gable-end location of the fireplace to be so attractive that they began to build other farmhouses in this manner. Another confirmation of this building procedure was made by F. A. Michaux, who traveled in Pennsylvania in 1802 and states that "these houses are made of trunks of trees, from twenty to thirty feet long, and four or five inches in diameter, placed one above the other, and supported by letting their ends into each other. . . . The chimney which is always at one of the ends is also made of trunks of trees of suitable length."

The chimneys that Michaux refers to are known as cobwork and were made by cutting short lengths of logs and laying them on top of each other as in the house itself. They were covered only with mud to minimize the danger of fire. Such chimneys must have imposed limitations on the size of the fire buring in these flammable surroundings.

Unfortunately, only one log house that was built during the seventeenth century in the Delaware Valley has survived. It is located in the borough of Prospect Park, and this cabin stands on the bank of Darby Creek (between Philadelphia and Chester). Now restored and open to the public, this ancient structure is evidence of the building techniques of the region, attributed largely to early Swedish and Finnish settlers. The original portion of this homestead was constructed near the middle of the seventeenth century by Morton Mortonson, great-grandfather of John Morton, a signer of the Declaration of Independence. About 1698 a second log house was erected nearby, and later the intervening space was enclosed with stone walls, thus creating one dwelling, as it were, with one continuous roof.

The joining of these two log houses is an example of a procedure followed throughout the New World. Due to limitations of time and resources, the first houses were of simple one-room design with a fireplace and a loft. As families grew and farmers became more affluent, additions were made to the original house. In the case of the Mortons they were joined end to end, although elsewhere others were joined crosswise.

The Mortonson homestead at Prospect Park, Pennsylvania. Courtesy of the Pennsylvania Historical and Museum Commission.

Deserted half-timber farmhouse near Wakefield, Pennsylvania.

Although trade with the Indians was an original intention of colonization in this area, farm dwellings and buildings were built near the river from Philadelphia southward. Lands were cleared and fields planted with grain and vegetables known in the homeland. To these, maize, pumpkin, squash, and other indigenous crops were eventually added. But despite grandiose trading and agricultural plans, chaos became a common pattern in the region, and little of substance was accomplished. There was incompetence and self-seeking among the leaders, and these traits, combined with lagging interest on the part of the settlers, prevented the colony from growing and solidifying. Eventually, it was taken over by the English.

A style of architecture exists in which both wood and masonry materials are used, known as half-timbered. Although this style was common in Europe from England to Bavaria, few such houses were built in America. Such construction included a framework of wood with angle braces at the corners, the interstices filled with stones or bricks and sometimes covered with plaster. In York, Pennsylvania, the Plough Tavern stands as a unique example of half-timbering, resting on a first-floor wall of logs. In the small farmhouse near Wakefield, Pennsylvania, pictured above, the opposite construction is found, with a second floor of logs topping a first floor of stone.

One would naturally expect to find many such examples of half-timbering in America, but there seems to have been a shift from frame construction directly to that of stone. It must be remembered, however, that, at least throughout the first half of the eighteenth century, log buildings far out-numbered those of stone. This proportion is not evident in farmhouses which survive, because the mortality rate in log houses has been high owing to fire, and also many have been completely covered with clapboards, thus concealing their original identities.

Often, the early colonists would take the land most conveniently at hand. Hence, the first settlements were along the Delaware River, while later colonists had to settle for less desirable spots without river frontage. Many had to go farther inland, and by the end of the seventeenth century some settlers were filtering through as far west as the present borough of West Chester, Pennsylvania.

One of the colonists who penetrated to the frontier in the late seventeenth century was William Brinton, along with his wife Ann Bagley. They came from Sedgeley Parish, Staffordshire, England, and settled in Birmingham Township, Chester County, Pennsylvania in 1684. There they built a one-story-high cabin, twenty-one by twenty-five feet, of poplar-wood planks, four inches thick. This house was occupied by the William Brinton family until the death of the parents in the very last years of the seventeenth century. A son, William Brinton, born in England, married Jane Thatcher in 1690, and built the 1704 Brinton house. Occupied by direct descendants until 1802, the family residence was awarded to Joseph Brinton, another line from the Brintons then living there. John Hill Brinton (1830—1892) was interested in family genealogy and interviewed many aged people who knew about the 1704 house. His entry in 1863 is very long and concludes: "I thus relate these facts minutely in order that some future Brinton, descended from the colonist, (if he so minds) may restore the house to its primitive aspect and plant memorial stones where these settlers rest."

When the builder William Brinton and his wife died, a complete inventory of the contents of the 1704 Brinton house was made, thereby helping the present generation of Brintons to faithfully furnish the house as it was originally.

This venerable edifice, standing near the West Chester–Wilmington turnpike, had undergone many changes before it was properly restored in the 1950s. It has survived so long, of course, because it was unusually well built. Its stone walls are twenty-two inches thick, some of the woodwork was of walnut, and the big timbers were hewn as smooth as can be done with a plane. The front door was originally made of three thicknesses of walnut, securely nailed together. The porch on the south elevation of the house has been replaced with side seats like the originals.

From diary notes and surviving evidence in the house itself, it is known that the original kitchen was located in one end of the cellar. In the other end were two rooms, one cold for the storage of root crops, the other a dry

The 1704 William Brinton house near West Chester, Pennsylvania.

cellar. Entrance to both could be made through an outside cellar door, an appendage often found on farmhouses. A hall and parlor occupied the first floor, three bedrooms the second floor.

In addition to the outside cellar door and the room for cold storage, there is other evidence that the 1704 Brinton house was a working farm for many years. The remnants of an early barn have been found, as have old foundations of other outbuildings. The barn most probably had a granary, since a nineteenth-century occupant reported that corn grew in the fields as high as twelve feet, and the lowest ears were so high that a man of average height could not reach them.

In the early eighteenth century the log house took on a new appearance, not developed from the Swedish antecedent, but initiated by a new ethnic group which took over the settling of southeastern Pennsylvania.

One would naturally think that the founding of Philadelphia, commonly known as a brick city at that time, would have influenced architecturally the thousands of immigrants who passed through on their way to the hinterlands—or the present counties of Lancaster, York, Berks, and Northampton. But the immigrants who debarked at Philadelphia headed for the back country, which was famous for walnut trees and limestone soil. Most of these people never saw a Swedish log house, and they went on to build log houses at a furious rate until the countryside was filled with Germanic-styled houses. The alleged derivation from the Swedish log house is refuted in Wertenbaker's book *The Founding of American Civilization, the Middle Colonies,* which states: "Certain writers have assumed that the Pennsylvania Germans learned to build log houses from the Swedish settlers on the lower Delaware, but the most cursory examination of these structures shows them to be German, not Swedish in their antecedents."

Wertenbaker then proceeds to point out that the corners of Pennsylvania houses were assembled by four methods, ranging from a crude saddle notch to a sophisticated dovetail joint. Many of these houses were about thirty feet by twenty feet and consisted of one room and a loft. Some towns were composed almost completely of log houses, including Abbotstown, Pennsylvania, and Hagerstown, Maryland, the latter being located only a few miles over the Maryland-Pennsylvania state line.

In describing these farmhouses as Germanic, one should point out that the houses and barns joined under one roof, found so frequently in Germany, apparently never were built there. Although a painting abroad by an unknown artist purports to represent the first house built in Bethlehem, Pennsylvania, to be the combination type, there is no documentary proof of the existence of the buildings. Of course other types of log houses are known to historians, and some of them were built there.

The hard work and frugality of these German immigrants have been well publicized and need no further elaboration. But as they prospered or as their families outgrew their simple one-room cabins, they put up new dwellings of logs, with a few added refinements. One change was to enlarge the overall

Combination house and barn allegedly built in 1741 at Bethlehem, Pennsylvania. Photo courtesy of J. Carroll Tobias.

size of their newly built home and divide the interior into two rooms. The loft was now reached by a more substantial stair than formerly. Such a development can be seen in the Bertolet-Herbein cabin on the site of the Daniel Boone homestead in Berks County, Pennsylvania. Creating two rooms required a major change in regard to the fireplace, which was then moved from a gable end to the wall partitioning the two structures. The most amazing aspect of this change was that the enormous fireplace faced into the smaller room, leaving the large room without any means of heat. Of course, there was a door between the two rooms and some heat would drift into the larger room through it.

Thus, the small room became the most important and warmest in the house. It contained the door to the outside as well as the staircase to the loft. It really was an all-purpose room, where cooking and eating took place and the daily chores of the household were performed. The fireplace and chimney were built of fieldstone and, like all colonial fireplaces, were highly inefficient when it came to the utilization of heat. The massive size of the fireplace suggests that several small fires might be burning at one time, with additional space in the corners for smoking meat or drying fruit. In addition, crafts were practiced here.

73

The Bertolet-Herbein cabin on the site of the Daniel Boone homestead in Berks County, Pennsylvania. Photo by Jack E. Boucher. Courtesy of the Historic American Buildings Survey.

First-floor plan of the Bertolet-Herbein cabin.

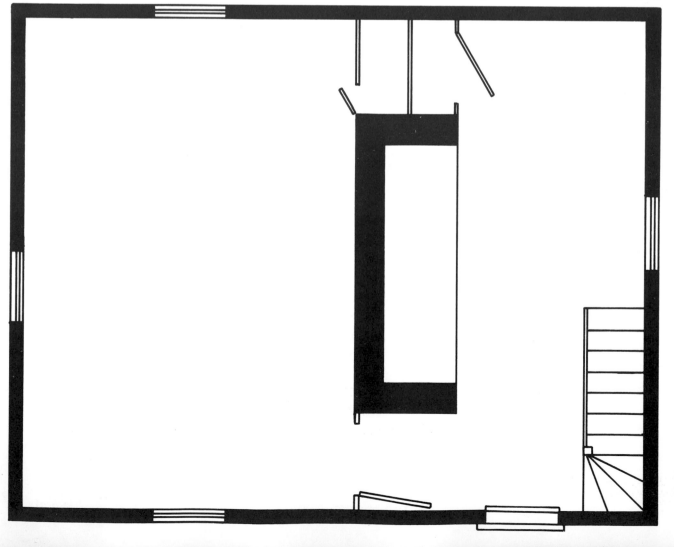

7 Pennsylvania

By mid-eighteenth century the round-log construction of farmhouses had been abandoned for skillfully hewn square logs with an inletting pattern resembling dovetails joints. This procedure reduced the size of the openings between the logs and resulted in a need for less chinking in order to keep the house warm. The plan of the house was changed again by further enlarging and dividing the interior into three rooms, with a loft or possibly an entire second floor. The long narrow room across one end was retained, and it continued to serve as an entry and kitchen. The remaining space on the first floor was no longer utilized as one big room but was built into two, providing a parlor and a bedroom. Often in the parlor wall, in the rear of the fireplace, an iron stove (five-plate jamb stove) was inserted, its fuel supplied from the fireplace in the adjoining kitchen and its smoke going up the kitchen chimney. The chimney was obviously off-center as it rose above the roof, and only in rare cases was there a second chimney on the far end.

Historians of architecture have pointed out that at the beginning of the century there were not only log cabins, but also stone cabins. These stone cabins were similar to the log ones in size, shape, and chimney. They were also more attractive, more comfortable, and more enduring, although it is difficult to find examples today. Recently a house was demolished which followed the two-room plan like the log house previously described, but this example was built against a hill, and thus one additional room in the cellar was above ground level. This plan is similar to that of bank barns, which are so plentiful in southeastern Pennsylvania today. Such a design was used for both houses and barns until the twentieth century, the lower part of the structures being warm in the winter and cool in the summer. Some of these small stone structures were expanded vertically with one full room on top of

Stone farmhouse built in 1767 by John de Turk in the Oley Valley, Berks County, Pennsylvania.

Stone cabin in Lebanon County, Pennsylvania. House is no longer standing.

The Christian Herr house located near Lancaster, Pennsylvania, was built in 1719. Courtesy of John Milner.

the other, and the basement may or may not have been exposed. The John de Turk house built in 1767 in the Oley Valley is an example of this latter type. John de Turk was a son of Isaac de Turk, a Huguenot who settled in Berks County in 1712 and was one of a number of French Protestant pioneers to settle in this area.

But perhaps more attention should be given to the Christian Herr house, one of the most important farmhouses of Pennsylvania. Completed by 1719, it is located about eight miles from the city of Lancaster, although the site of the city was not determined until 1729, when Lancaster County was established. It lies near the Great Conestoga Road, the main thoroughfare from the Susquehanna River to Philadelphia before the Lancaster-Philadelphia turnpike was built late in the eighteenth century.

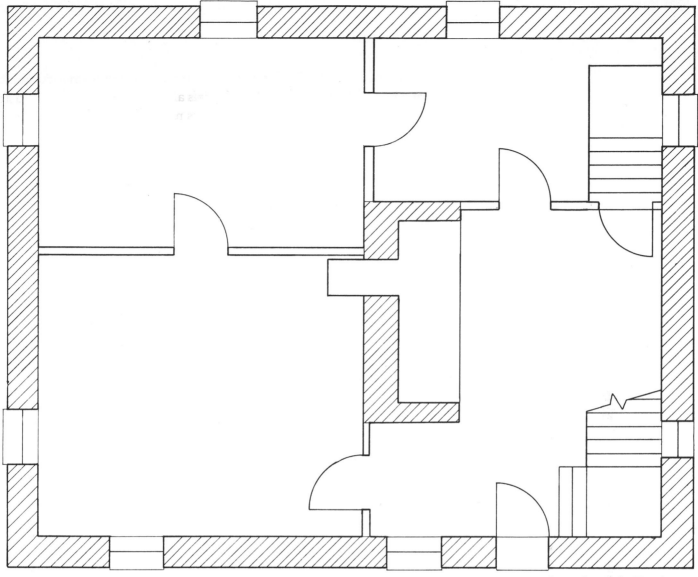

First-floor plan of the Herr house.

The story of the Herr farmhouse begins with the early settlements in Lancaster County. According to I. Daniel Rupp in *A History of Lancaster County* (published in 1844):

> About the year 1706 or 1707, a number of persecuted Swiss Mennonites went to England, and made particular agreement with the Honourable Proprietor, William Penn, at London, for lands to be taken up. Several families from the Palatinate, descendants of the distressed Swiss, emigrated to America and settled in Lancaster County in the year 1709.

Subsequently a warrant was issued for 10,000 acres of land near the Pequea Creek, twenty miles east of the town of Conestoga. This tract was later broken down into smaller ones, and each new owner was required to *lodge a family* within three years after the purchase was made. It is known that this mandate was not strictly enforced.

In 1711 Christian Herr bought a tract of 539 acres and built his home on it. He carved his initials and the date, 1719, into the sandstone lintel of the front door. Herr's house is notable for a number of reasons. In the first place, it is the oldest farmhouse standing in Lancaster County and one of the oldest in Pennsylvania. Of no less importance is its pure Germanic form of architecture. During recent preservation work on the house, a study was made of prototypes in Germany, and a number were found which were similar. In addition, it is a very large house. Not only did the house serve as an integral part of the farm, but also it was used for Mennonite services for a hundred years.

The exterior of this farmhouse has a number of striking features. It was obviously built of fieldstone, a logical resource when there were so many demands on the time and skills of the workmen. It was also very economical, for the stones were gathered from the surface of the ground and roughly fitted together without any chipping or forming. It is very evident that the Herr farmhouse was built by skillful workmen, for after two and a half centuries the walls are still in reasonably good condition, although they were repointed when the house was restored. Exposure to the air has colored some stones very deeply, producing a pleasing contrast in the masonry.

Another striking feature is the "double attic," which consists of two attic floors within the gable roof of the house. Such an arrangement was also an economical measure, since, generally speaking, the roof was less costly to construct than the stone wall of a second story. Few other farmhouses of this region have double attics like this one.

The small size of the windows should also be noted. This medieval feature is to be found in a few other houses in this area. The panes of the windows are small, due to the high cost and scarcity of large panes of glass. The lower sections of the windows are hinged and swing inward, a feature commonly found in Germanic architecture. Window openings are surrounded with stone sills, stiles, and lintels, the stiles having two holes drilled into them to accept the pintles of shutter hinges. The shutters consist of a number of small boards mounted vertically on two horizontal battens. All of these features were designed to withstand intruders and the cold.

The off-center location of the chimney and the front door give a clue to the floor plan on the inside, a common pattern for Germanic-styled domestic architecture. In some cases the door leads directly into a long room laid crosswise. It is possible that such an arrangement prevailed at one time, but subsequently a bedroom was created from part of the kitchen. The immense fireplace in the kitchen suggests a very large room, much larger than the present one. A growing family, however, might have created a demand for a first-floor bedroom and could well have forced a change in the utilization of space. Old people could get into this bedroom without climbing stairs, for example, and heat in the kitchen could reach this adjacent bedchamber.

The importance of the kitchen or all-purpose room in the Herr farmhouse warrants attention. Its main function was the preparation and serving of food; however, its giant fireplace was probably never filled with long logs, but, as is the case with other fireplaces that were built during this period, a number of small fires were built simultaneously in order to prepare different dishes for the table. An adjoining oven is absent, because it was a Germanic custom to set them up outside the main house. A few such examples have survived, an outstanding one at the Cloister at Ephrata, Pennsylvania. Such a location had obvious advantages in the summer and equally obvious disadvantages in the winter.

Because the fireplace was the only source of heat (and of light in the evenings), much activity was centered around it. Threads could be spun, candles poured, and mending stitched by women, while men repaired harnesses or wheels, particularly in the winter, when outdoor chores could hardly be performed.

The layout of the Herr farmhouse indicates that the rest of the first floor was divided into two rooms: One served as a parlor called a *stube*, the other a bedchamber, called a *zimmer*. These rooms were very similar in size and shape, the major difference being a high masonry stove in the parlor. This stove was connected to the back wall of the fireplace by two flues, one at the bottom for heat to enter, and one at the top as an exit for the smoke and provider of draft for the hot air to circulate. Without circulation little heat would have been drawn into the facility. Presumably, this stove was adequate to heat the parlor, despite the fact that it was located at the end of the room, whence only limited convection of currents could dissipate the heat.

Gigantic fireplace in the Herr house. Courtesy of John Milner.

The Abiah Taylor farmhouse near West Chester, Pennsylvania.

A winding stairway located in a corner of the kitchen leads to the second floor, and another with steps made of hewn timbers rises from the second to the third. There is one fireplace on the second floor. Under part of the house is a vaulted cellar, which was used for the traditional storage of meat and produce. A stairway from the kitchen leads to the cellar. Curiously, there is no evidence of an outer cellar entrance, this omission perhaps having been a safety precautuion.

But this edifice of the Mennonite patriarch must not be regarded as typical of its time and place and was probably an awesome sight for less fortunate settlers who lived nearby in cabins made of log or stone. These were warm and comfortable but lacked the size and refinements of the ancient stone mansion. It, like many other restored farmhouses today, shows virtually no evidence of being a farmhouse, for the furnishings and the outbuildings are missing. There are no baskets or crocks in the kitchen and no oven or smokehouse in the backyard. It is to be hoped that these will eventually receive full attention as the restoration continues. The farmhouse is now open to the public six days a week.

A chronological evolution of Pennsylvania farmhouses leads to a discussion of the Abiah Taylor house, in Chester County. Chester County was one of the first three counties simultaneously established in Pennsylvania by William Penn, the others being Philadelphia and Bucks. The Taylor farmhouse, constructed in 1724, is located in East Bradford Township near the Philadelphia-Lancaster road, two miles from the borough of West Chester.

Abiah Taylor, the original owner, was born in Didcott, Berkshire, England. He married Deborah Gearing of Farington Meeting (Quaker) in the same county in 1694. They emigrated to Pennsylvania about 1702 and presumably built a log cabin on the site where the present brick farmhouse of 1724 stands. However, there is no documented record of such a building, nor have any of its remains survived.

Much information about the Taylor farmstead has been taken from two entries in local newspapers. The first entry "A public Sale of Real Estate," appeared in *The Village Record*, West Chester, Pennsylvania, February 9, 1831. This entry gives the location of the property and mentions the owners of land adjoining the farm. Among the improvements were a brick house facing southward, a stone springhouse, and a limekiln. The farm consisted of 220 acres, divided into convenient fields and enclosed by substantial fences. About 58 acres were in woodland, principally hickory and black oak. A vein of limestone, where a quarry could be opened with little difficulty, combined with an adequate supply of stone for the limekiln. A fine stream of water, adequate for a meadow of 30 to 40 acres increased the value of the land. It was described as a very healthy estate and in a good neighborhood near mills, schools, and places of worship. It was, indeed, one of the most handsome farms in Chester County.

A second account, called "A Relic," by John Reuben appeared in the *Daily Local News*, West Chester, Pennsylvania, January 20, 1883. Mr. Reuben mentions the location of the house and then proceeds to point out that its bricks were made from a nearby clay pit, that it was built on a mound sloping all around but now disfigured on the west side by an abrupt cut in the public road. He states that at that time the house was in excellent condition, and compares its longevity to the Egyptian pyramids. Most importantly, he describes a section of a leaded window sash which was taken from the Taylor house. He notes that on the west side there are four windows on the north, two very small ones, also with leaded sash. He said, "I have portions of the sash referred to, and it was brought from England." Taylor's other possession, says Reuben, was an oaken chest in which his family brought their wardrobe, but Reuben surmises that the chest was not large enough to hold the pants of a family of his own time.

A close examination of the Taylor house reveals that it is still in sound condition today. The floor plan has been changed little, except that a stone kitchen was added on the east side sometime in the eighteenth century. The 1798 direct tax of the Internal Revenue Department shows that a stone kitchen eighteen by twenty-one feet was attached, thus closing an outside entry into the cellar. In the original kitchen a trapdoor gives access to the partial cellar under the house. The one chimney is located in the north wall

Datestone of the Taylor farmhouse.

Three small windows in the north wall of the Taylor house.

and possesses a common flue for the various fireplaces. Also in the north wall are three small windows, one in a first-floor closet, another in the stairs, and the third in a second-floor bedroom. Although the leaden sash has been removed, the openings appear to be intact.

The first floor retains its original two rooms. However, the one large cooking fireplace has been considerably reduced in size, it being no longer necessary as a source of heat. The stairway is in its original position, but has been rebuilt with new lumber. On the second floor the large north bedroom remains as do two smaller ones. The small fireplaces on the second floor of the house have been closed, and only the attic retains its original floorboards.

The author examined the house before reading comments about it and observed that the bricks retained excellent color, with the mortar virtually intact. The bricks were laid in Flemish bond. The water table is at its proper height around the house and is made of bricks precisely formed for that purpose. The bricks are segmentally arranged over the cellar windows, although the openings are partially covered and are beginning to deteriorate. All told, the house is in remarkable condition, which can be accounted for by the expert workmanship of the builders.

Little evidence exists to suggest that it was specifically designed as a farmhouse. Most farmhouses in the eighteenth century had outer entrances, which, however, are also found on city houses of the same era. The inside trapdoor would suggest that the cellar was used for "cold storage" after the outer door was permanently closed. The original large fireplace might be regarded as a farm necessity. Only the presence of outbuildings—now completely missing—could attest to the fact that the Taylor place was a farmhouse.

Its real virtue in this survey is the fact that it is a small house, influenced by English medieval architecture and occupied by an English yeoman. It was the sort of house immigrants dreamed about, but certainly very few owned. It must have been one of the first substantial houses built in Chester County, and its survival is evidence of the care given to it. However, it will need some help to last another two and a half centuries.

By looking at a map of Pennsylvania, one can easily understand why early settlements were made along the Delaware River, south of Philadelphia. After Philadelphia was established, immigrants landed there and fanned out toward the hinterland. There was rich farmland to the west, and two houses have been discussed that stand in Chester County, both of which were built in the first quarter of the eighteenth century. Instead of pushing farther westward from Philadelphia, the next trend was toward the north, and fine farmhouses were built in Bucks County throughout the eighteenth century.

There were limits to the distance of the frontier that farmers could penetrate. In the first place, many wanted to stay as near to Philadelphia as possible, for there they secured goods which their rural economy could not produce. They needed glass for their windows, tools for their farms, and Bibles for their religious meetings. Secondly, toward the north lay Indian territory, and few farmers relished the thought of fighting Indians while trying to farm fields.

Among the houses built in Bucks County is the small Bennet-Search house in Northampton Township. It is known that Abraham Bennet bought several acres of land in 1687; however, the date of the first house is thought to be 1744.

As was the practice in other areas, the original Bennet house was very small, approximately eighteen by twenty-three feet. It was built of fieldstone and is now nicely pointed. However, when Dr. H. C. Mercer, of the Bucks County Historical Society, examined the property in 1919, he felt that the walls originally may have been plastered on the outside or that the pointing may have been carelessly smeared over the joints. There are two stories and a loft, with a winding stairway reaching from the cellar to the attic.

The interior is reasonably well lighted by two windows on the first floor; there was probably at least one window in the west wall, which is now covered by the larger second portion of the house. The windows on the first floor have nine panes over six, while those on the second floor have six over six. There is a small window on the first floor to light a small pantry that

The Bennet-Search farmhouse before restoration, in Northampton Township, Bucks County, Pennsylvania. Courtesy of Robert D. Crompton.

filled the space between the jamb of the fireplace and the outside wall. In this pantry survives a sink, hollowed out of one large piece of stone.

A cooking fireplace is located in the east wall of the house with a nine-foot lintel. A beehive oven was originally located outside the house but connected with the inside—entry to it being through the back wall of the fireplace.

One outstanding feature of the smaller part of the house is found on the second floor. There a small fireplace is surrounded with paneling, which seems very sophisticated when compared with the general architectural tone of the house.

The chair rails on both the first and second floors are original. And handwrought nails were used throughout the house, suggesting that it was constructed during the eighteenth century. Mercer reported that in both sections of the house the rafters of the second floor were exposed, all having beaded edges.

Formerly, the Bennet-Search farmhouse was flanked by several appending buildings, including a three-story, stone wagon shed, a massive Dutch barn that was struck by lightning and burned many years ago, and a cave cellar, about seventy-five feet southeast of the house. The cave cellar survives in excellent condition and is pictured in the chapter about cave cellars.

It is commonly thought that the second part of the house was built in the last decade of the eighteenth century. The first floor consists of two parallel rooms, one end butting against the old house, the other end terminating in an attractive hall running crosswise through the house. There are corner fireplaces in each of these rooms, with details reminiscent of the Federal period. There is a chimney in the outside wall of the hall, but no fireplace. It is possible that a freestanding Franklin stove was used there, with a pipe attached to the chimney flue. At the end opposite the entry a graceful, curving staircase leads to the second floor. Just before World War II, when the house was not occupied, vandals entered and stole the corner mantels of the new wing. Later, these were retrieved from an antique shop and restored to their original locations.

The house was owned by the Bennets during the eighteenth and early nineteenth centuries and thereafter by members of the Search family, who are actually descendants of the Bennet family; hence, its name, the Bennet-Search farmhouse. Presently, it is called "Hampton-Hill." It was named a National Historic Landmark on June 5, 1973. Its present owners and occupants are Mr. and Mrs. Robert D. Crompton.

Western Pennsylvania was frontier country in the late eighteenth century. In 1783 the German traveler Johann David Schoepf wrote, "Pittsburgh at this time numbers perhaps 60 wooden houses and cabins, in which live something more than 100 families, for by the outbreak of the last war, the growth of the place beginning to be rapid, was hindered." A cabin in point is the one in which William Holmes McGuffey was born in 1780. Originally, it was located on a farm of 400 acres, in Washington County, Pennsylvania,

Front view of the restored Bennet-Search house. Courtesy of Robert D. Crompton.

Beautiful winding stairs
in the Bennet-Search house.

First-floor plan of the Bennet-Search farmhouse.

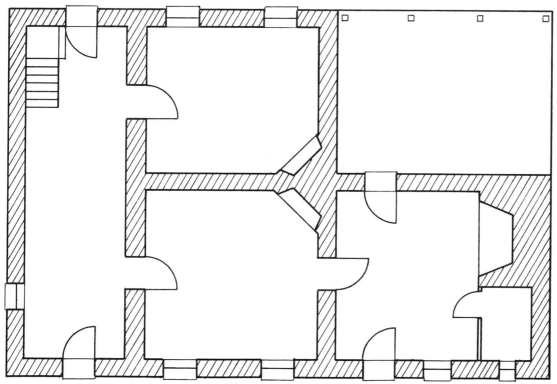

William H. McGuffey farmhouse originally built in Washington County, Pennsylvania, and reconstructed in the Henry Ford Museum. Courtesy of the Henry Ford Museum, Dearborn, Michigan.

Interior of the William H. McGuffey farmhouse. Courtesy of the Collections of the Henry Ford Museum, Dearborn, Michigan.

but today the cabin has been relocated and refurbished in the Henry Ford Museum in Dearborn, Michigan.

Its windows are small, but the door seems to be about the same size as doors of today. One of the outstanding features of the cabin is an outside ladder to the loft. Such an arrangement would lead one to believe that it was only used for storage. The original appending farm buildings included a barn and a smokehouse.

The inside walls of the cabin were not plastered, and the beam ceiling is exposed, as was customary. The fireplace is built of stone, with a large stone lintel in lieu of the wooden type used on the Eastern seaboard.

The furnishings of the house, aside from a butter churn and flax wheel, are very sophisticated for a primitive dwelling. Most of the furniture is eighteenth-century and would be more logically found in a dwelling in the East. There is a great deal of lathe work involved in making the furniture, particularly in the bed, candlestand, table, chairs, and spinning wheel. There is even some in the cradle.

The famous McGuffey was born in this cabin in 1800 and was educated in a local school. At other times he was taught by his parents or neighbors. It is said that a clergyman passing the house heard his mother pray that her children might be educated, and arranged for McGuffey to attend the Old Stone Academy at Darlington, Pennsylvania.

He later worked his way through Washington and Jefferson College in Washington, Pennsylvania. From 1826 to 1836 he taught at Miami University at Oxford, Ohio, and at that time launched his famous readers. He did much to influence the moral and cultural development of thousands of American children. From 1845 to 1873 McGuffey taught at the University of Virginia, at Charlottesville. He died May 4, 1873.

Meanwhile, considerable growth occurred near the oldest inland town in America, namely, Lancaster. The Martin farmstead, which is located in Manor Township in Lancaster County, lies in a rich limestone area southwest of Lancaster, midway between the city and the Susquehanna River. Although the farmhouse was built in 1805, stylistically it precedes that time by at least twenty-five years. Originally the farm consisted of 259 acres, but today it is a working farm of about 100 acres.

The Martin farm is a unique example among those in Lancaster County. In the first place, the house is quite large, thirty by thirty-four feet. The demands made on the house were varied. A spacious kitchen was needed to prepare large quantities of food for daily consumption, as well as for winter storage. In addition, a sick lamb or baby chickens might share the quarters for a few days. Also, farm families, themselves, have been traditionally large, particularly in Pennsylvania, where any number from six to twelve has not been uncommon. If the farming family was small, it is likely that "hired hands" were brought in for several days at a time, and additional accommodations were necessary for eating and sleeping. Often the oldest child married and "lived in," until suitable quarters could be arranged. The oldest son might inherit a new farm, although the division of the parents' assets were not usually made until the death of the father.

Little is known about Johannes and Anne Hersche, the builders of this farmhouse. They were of Germanic ancestry, as is evidenced by the datestones—one in German and the other in English—on the house. The use of the datestones on houses was a common practice in rural Pennsylvania; less frequently, they are found on barns. These stones are a permanent record of the year in which the house was built and also, add a slight decorative touch. It is further known that the Hersches were Mennonites, and for a time, there was a threat of their being excluded from the church because they had built such a "fancy" house.

The house is really grand and beautiful. Its evenly balanced facade and the interior arrangement of rooms stamps it as pure English Georgian. A center hall, from the front door to the back door, is reduced in width toward the rear, by a staircase that reaches from the first floor to the attic. Two rooms are placed on each side of the hall, on the first floor. A large fireplace has survived in the back room on the left side, and this room originally was the kitchen. The fireplace is simply designed and accented with trim and a mantel shelf, on which antique china and pewterware were displayed. The fireplace chamber has the usual crane, from which boiling pots could be removed after the crane was swung forward over the hearth. In the opposite wall there is a low door providing entry into a small closet under the hall stairs. The outside door of the kitchen is known as an "Indian" door, because there is a sliding panel on the bottom part that could be raised over the glass section at the top. This panel, of course, was used to provide protection against marauders and also the stinging cold of long winter nights. Solid shutters on the windows of the first floor served the same purposes.

Across the hall from the kitchen is a spacious bedroom with a small fireplace built into the corner, but flat against the wall instead of the usual diagonal position. It is very simply treated, for in comparison to the parlor and the kitchen it was a less important room. Its location did not permit easy observation of activities at the barn, but its convenience to the kitchen had its advantages.

The doors of the house, which are architecturally compatible with the features of the house, are nicely proportioned and fitted with attractive panels. In addition, all are fitted with Germanic iron-rim locks. These have barlike handles for opening and are reputed to be the only locks a person can open with both hands occupied. They are sometimes called *elbow locks*, for they are opened by the elbow pressing on them and drawing the door open. The German lock on the front door is an unusually large example. Strap hinges reach across the entire width of the door. This procedure was

Farmstead of Mr. and Mrs. Jacob Martin near Lancaster, Pennsylvania, was built in 1805 by Johannes and Anna Hersche.

followed to keep the door from sagging after many years of use. It functions as well today as it did when originally installed.

The cellar is only half the size of the house, with doors on the inside and outside. It was particularly important to have a large outside door for the easy storing of fruits and vegetables.

The summerhouse at the rear of the main house, although originally a separate entity, is now joined to the house. Although quite small in comparison with the main house, during the summer it was the center of farm life. It was equipped with a large fireplace that was used for the daily preparation of food, for baking, and for boiling soap and apple butter. An oven outside the wall of the summerhouse was completely enclosed except for an iron door that was mounted to the back wall of the fireplace. Through this door coals were placed in the oven to heat it for baking, and after the hot coals were removed, the baking goods were inserted on a long-handled tool called a peel. Baking was done once or twice a week.

There is one discordant feature on the exterior of this house, namely the front porch. Porches were not in common use when the house was built, nor

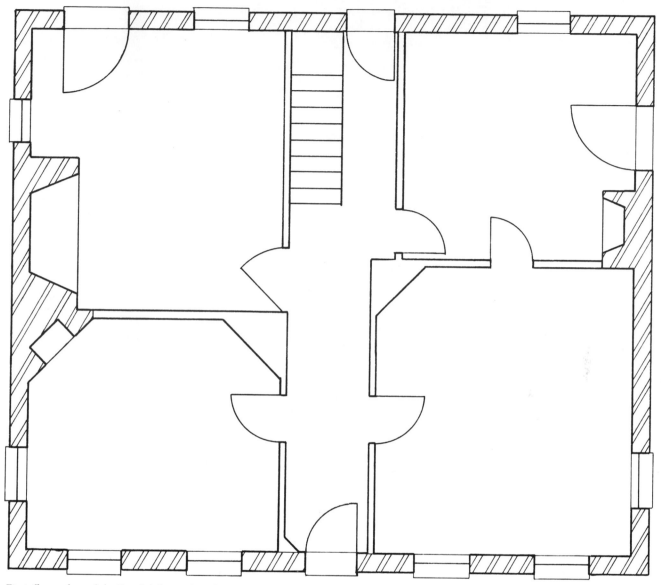

First-floor plan of the Jacob Martin farmhouse.

is there evidence that it was a later addition. But it is doubtful that the skilled men who built this charming house would have contrived such clumsy porch posts, which seem so incompatible with other details of the house. Also, new window sashes were placed in the lower half of the windows—an obvious attempt to update the house when a newer style window became fashionable.

The Martin farmhouse originally had the usual complement of out-buildings, such as a smokehouse, a privy, a springhouse, and possibly an icehouse. All these were required to operate a well-regulated farm at the beginning of the nineteenth century. A well was dug near the kitchen door with a wooden pump to raise water when it was needed. Today, water is obtained from a nearby spring and pumped to the house with an electric pump. The huge barn stands about two hundred feet from the house amidst smaller buildings, such as a tobacco shed and a pigsty.

Porch columns on the Jacob Martin farmhouse.

One wonders how Johannes Hersche, supposedly a typical Mennonite farmer—unlettered but industrious and frugal—acquired the wealth to build such a fine house in the wilderness of Lancaster County. And was the house a brainchild of an architect or of a smart master carpenter? These questions may never be answered, although this house will continue to give pleasure to future generations.

Many of the farmhouses that were built in the last half of the eighteenth century on the Eastern seaboard followed the dictates of Georgian architecture. Gradually, this style was adopted as far west as Ohio during the early part of the nineteenth century. The Georgian-styled farmhouses were commodious, pleasant, and compatible with the economy of the period. But, as is often the case with man's achievements, the virtues of an era are quickly discarded in favor of new, different ideas, which are not necessarily better.

Thus, in the early years of the nineteenth century, farmhouse architecture in Pennsylvania began to follow a new trend, known as Federal. It was a later and more *simple* form of Federal, for one rarely finds round or oval rooms or, for that matter, Palladian windows. The central hall was continued but cut to half its original depth and came to an end at the foot of the stairs. The space to the rear was more carefully utilized. For example, in a farmhouse near York, Pennsylvania, the back end of the hall was absorbed by the kitchen area. The hall also became narrower but better lighted, for on each side of the door narrow panes of glass were installed, often with a fanlight or a transom overhead.

The size of the rooms often was reduced, and the trims on the windows and doors became less ornamented. Fireplaces were complemented with simple mantels. The rooms continued to be well lighted, often with three windows in each room. In a house near Carlisle in Cumberland County, the windows on the first floor have nine panes over six, on the second floor six over six.

On the exterior above the windows the straight or segmental brick header was replaced with a large wooden lintel, which was cheaper but obviously less attractive. Water tables were generally dropped; however, a simple sawtooth cornice often ran across the front and rear walls of brick houses. Small porches became fashionable, although they were but an embryonic form of those of the Greek Revival period that followed.

The chimneys usually indicate the locations of the fireplaces, which were flat against an outside wall, pinched in a corner between a window and a partition between the rooms. Fireplaces shrank in size, for with the flaring jambs of the era, they became more effective in heating rooms. Andirons were shortened to fit into the smaller fireplaces.

In the style and construction details of the house near Carlisle there is nothing that indicates that it is or was part of a working farm of about a hundred acres. However, just a few steps from the side backdoor stands a summerhouse with a front porch running across its entire width and a typical fireplace. Next to the summerhouse stands a smokehouse, and beyond is a large bank barn (a barn built into the side of a hill) along with a few smaller outbuildings.

Styles changed rapidly in the next fifty years. Next, the abbreviated hall was eliminated altogether, leaving only four rooms on the first floor. This procedure was a more economical use of space, but it did eliminate the privacy that was possible by using a hall.

The function of these four rooms is somewhat of a mystery, for no floor plan is known to exist that identifies them. It seems safe to assume, however, that one of the front rooms served as a parlor, and one of the back rooms was undoubtedly used as a kitchen. And it is probable that the other back room was used as a dining room, and the remaining front room used as a family sitting room.

The elimination of the hall meant that if only one door was provided, traffic destined for the parlor must necessarily pass through the sitting room, or the sitting room traffic would have to enter through the parlor. This

Federal-styled farmhouse built near Carlisle, Pennsylvania.

Victorian farmhouse of David Mayer, built in Lancaster, Pennsylvania, in 1867.

dilemma was easily solved by furnishing the house with two front doors.

There has been considerable conjecture about the purposes of the parlor door. Some folklorists claim that it existed primarily to allow a bride to be carried across its threshold. Others claim that it served as a funeral door and was used only when caskets were carried out of the house. It is a fact, however, that two front doors were common occurrences, one used primarily by the family, the other used primarily on Sundays, holidays, and by guests. Parenthetically, it might be mentioned that the author has lived in three houses that had two front doors.

The last farmhouse style in Pennsylvania to be considered is Victorian. Architecturally, the style is thought of as eclectic, because so many of its facets were borrowed from earlier styles, including Romanesque, Gothic, Classical, and Georgian. The mid-nineteenth century was a period of change and expansion, a period that tried to combine new ideas with what was thought to be the best of older concepts.

The Mayer farmhouse, built on the north side of Lancaster in 1867, is an unusual example of farmhouse architecture. Although it is obviously a Victorian structure, it lacks many features commonly associated with that style. Its extended cornice, supported by pairs of brackets, makes the house look strong and substantial (as it really is). The unusually large porch with its posts bracketed at the top is typically Victorian. And, the porte cochere adds elegance to an already imposing residence. The floor plan is largely Georgian, having a central hall along with two gigantic rooms on either side, each, however, with Victorian-styled fireplaces. Towards the rear of the house is attached a large kitchen, under which is the largest root cellar ever encountered by the author. The cupola on top of the roof completes this graceful Victorian farmhouse.

8 Ohio

It is not as easy to classify the architectural styles of Ohio farmhouses as it is for farmhouses along the Eastern seacoast, where the earliest architectural styles followed the ethnic origins of the settlers. There was some intermixture in the styles of construction, but for the most part, the first permanent houses reflected the contemporary architectural patterns of England, Sweden, Holland, and Germany. A log cabin with a fireplace located in a corner indicated a Swedish influence, while a fireplace that was placed in the center of the gable end wall showed a German influence. There was neither time nor inclination to drastically change the architectural pattern of one's homeland.

In Ohio, the situation is different. Here, the major architectural influences are described as deriving from New England, New York, Pennsylvania, Maryland, and Virginia, and consequently, farmhouses are classified according to the American origins of the settlers. In the event that the settlers emigrated directly from Europe, as thousands did, they erected farmhouses that were architecturally similar and compatible with those already built. As late as 1870, as many as 45 percent of the population of Holmes County, Ohio, is known to have come from Germany. In the *Nicholas Joss Letters*, a German immigrant in the early 1830s tells how he and his group left their homeland and sailed for New York City. Arriving there, they transferred to a ship bound for Albany, where they boarded another boat croassing New York State to Buffalo via the Erie Canal. In Buffalo, on Lake Erie, they engaged passage on a ship bound for Cleveland, where they disembarked and traveled overland to Holmes County. There they joined Amish people who had come from Pennsylvania, the majority of the families building log dwellings as they had known in Germany.

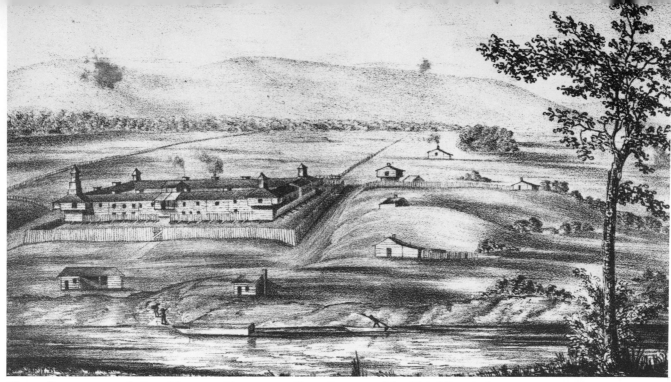

The earliest structures built at Marietta, Ohio, were of log. Courtesy of the Ohio Historical Society, Columbus, Ohio.

Architectural historians recognize a further intermixing of house styles in Ohio. For example, houses exhibiting Southern influences were built in northern Ohio, while houses with Northern influences were built in southern Ohio. I. T. Frary observes in his book *Early Homes of Ohio* that the state was a real melting pot of American architectural styles.

Styles were also modified and eliminated. The author has never encountered a saltbox house in Ohio, nor does Frary list this entry in the index of his book, although a few are now known to exist. Nor are there any large Virginia plantation houses, like Carter's Grove, Westover, or Shirley. Possibly Adena, near Chillicothe, comes the closest to a Virginia-styled plantation house, but after traveling in various parts of the state, one can understand that conditions such as uncleared land, hilly terrains, and small land plots, were not conducive to the plantation mode of living.

Settlement came to Ohio at least a century after that of the Eastern states. And as styles moved across the mountains, they had to be again adapted to frontier life, a mode of living that had generally disappeared in the East. Early houses in Ohio were no larger than necessary, and all of them were built of indigenous materials. Although double-hung windows were available in Philadelphia at the beginning of the eighteenth century, it is doubtful that they were available in Ohio for another quarter- or half-century. The materials used for house construction were brick, stone, and wood, although wood was predominantly used. Bricks were used in the nineteenth century, since Ohio is so rich in clays. Stone farmhouses, however, of the first half of the nineteenth century are a rarity.

There is no doubt that the earliest farm cabins in Ohio were built of logs. Sketches of early buildings in Marietta and of reconstructed ones in Schoenbrunn are examples of this practice, which was a very economical one to follow. A prospective farmer bought a parcel of land, covered with forests, and as he cleared his land he laid usable logs aside until he had enough to build a house. Then, with the help of his neighbors, he constructed a rectangular pen of logs in a matter of days. The farmer then could, by himself, cut the openings into his house, build his chimney of stone or cobwork, and make the necessary partitions within the house. The earliest cabins had earthen floors, and most of them had a loft overhead that was used for storage or emergency sleeping quarters. These log cabins were primitive, but very satisfactory, for many have outlasted houses built of other materials of a later period. As a matter of fact, hundreds have survived in Ohio, hidden in most cases by an outer coating of clapboard.

The reconstructed log cabins at Schoenbrunn (1772) are of interest, chiefly because many are more primitive than those that were built earlier in Pennsylvania. The smallest cabins were built without windows or a chimney. A smoke hole can be found in the roof, under which sits a crude tripod of heavy limbs, supporting an iron kettle. It seems probable that only a minimal amount of cooking could be done with such an arrangement, although some baking could be done by tucking food into the outer edges of the fire.

Reconstructed log cabin at Schoenbrunn, Ohio.

Some of the more orthodox cabins were built with doors and windows and an interesting chimney. The base of the chimney was composed of fieldstones, probably cemented with mud mortar, the balance being cob-work, consisting of sticks carefully stacked one upon the other, with interlocking corners, and a coating of mud mortar on the inside. Later, lean-tos were added to some of the cabins for the dry storage of wood. On at least two inner walls of the cabin lower shelves were built and covered with skins to provide bedding for the occupants. None of the cabins is very large (approximately fourteen by fifteen feet), so they would have been adequately heated by the open fireplace.

The diary of David Zeisberger, the Moravian leader of some Indians in Ohio, provides insight into the operation of an early Schoenbrunn farming community. It appears that the Indians came to the site with farming equipment, such as plows, harrows, about seventy Schoenbrunn head of cattle, and an equal number of horses. Oxen were the favorite beasts of burden in early settlements, because they required no expensive harnesses, were docile and easy to train, did not eat grain to survive, and were edible. Horses needed grain and therefore took food from the mouths of the settlers. Zeisberger reports that, the Indian women worked in the fields, while the men hunted. Corn was the major constituent of their diet, and upon their arrival they quickly cleared fields to plant it. The kernels could be dried, fried, roasted, or ground into meal in a primitive stone or wood mortar. It is likely that their diet was varied a bit by beans and pumpkins, particularly because these two vegetables could be planted among the cornstalks. It is interesting to note that Zeisberger taught the Indian children, wrote a book for them in the Indian language, and was their staunch friend until the site was abandoned in the confusion of later wars.

Although log cabins and houses are generally considered a primitive type of shelter, at least one elaborate, sophisticated one was built near Chillicothe, Ohio, according to descriptions by one of the occupants. Thomas Worthington's daughter, Sarah, who describes her home in *The Private Memoirs of Thomas Worthington, Esq.*, writes that the house was built of hewed logs (in 1802), and the chinking plaster was whitened by lime on the inside and outside. There were two large pens (complete log squares built separately) eighteen feet square, and a story and a half high. The space between them was enclosed with weatherboarding (probably clapboards), and the inner walls were plastered. The rooms were furnished with furniture brought from Virginia, made of mahogany and cherry wood. There was carpeting on the floors and curtains at the windows. Her father had a library, with one bed for hospitality, and her mother also had a room for her activities. There were additional rooms for servants—a story and a half high—with bedrooms in the lofts. The house was seven or eight rooms long in a direct line. This house was called Belleview and was eventually replaced by the present stone mansion, Adena, located near Chillicothe, Ohio.

As farmers living in log cabins became more prosperous, they had a number of options in regard to improving their living conditions. Some probably added a small appendage or two with cellars beneath for storing root crops. The rooms above the ground were used for dry storage or for bedrooms.

Another option was to build a two-and-a-half-story structure of logs. These were often made of carefully hewed logs, providing smaller cracks for chinking, sometimes covered with laths and plastered on the inside. Log houses are considered to be larger and more fastidiously finished buildings than cabins, and a sizable number of such farmhouses have no doubt survived in Ohio. The author found a deserted one, obviously verging on ruin, in Holmes County, Ohio. The location and size of the openings suggested a reasonably modern arrangement of rooms. At one side a disheveled springhouse was still supplying water, as it had done for a hundred years or more. I would hazard a guess that this house was built during the middle of the nineteenth century.

A third option was for the farmer to build a new house of wood, brick, or stone against one of the walls of his log cabin. After cutting doors, the log cabin could continue to serve as a summer kitchen for making soap or for butchering cattle and hogs in the fall of the year and then cooking and preserving their meat.

The final option was for the farmer to completely forget about his earlier abode and start from scratch at a new location, probably better suited for his needs than his first choice. There is no doubt that many followed such a procedure, and they are the ones whose houses can be observed today on the Ohio countryside.

It has been previously mentioned that during this period another style of building farmhouses prevailed, known as half-timber, or in German as *Fachwerk*. This type of construction, of which surviving examples are quite rare east of the Allegheny Mountains, is found more frequently in Ohio. Hubert G. H. Wilhelm and Michael Miller made a survey, principally in Holmes County, and found thirteen houses, one addition to a log house, and one barn in which this technique was used. Their findings were published in *Pioneer America*, July 1974. The writer photographed three such houses on his visit to Holmes County and the surrounding regions.

Although this type of construction is very common in various parts of Europe and is found in both cities and country areas, its use as an early type of construction in Ohio seems very unusual. It is thought that most of these houses were built during the first half of the nineteenth century, when pioneering was the common mode of living in rural areas. Its use is particularly interesting because so much more skill was required of the builders than was demanded of those who built log cabins and houses. At every intersection of the timber there was joinery and fitting to be done, techniques that demanded skills comparable to those of a cabinetmaker.

The corner posts ran from the sill to the roof plate, and all horizontal

Log cabin with appendages at the front and the rear. Located on the farm of John L. Beachy, near Berlin, Ohio.

First-floor plan of log cabin on the John L. Beachy farm.

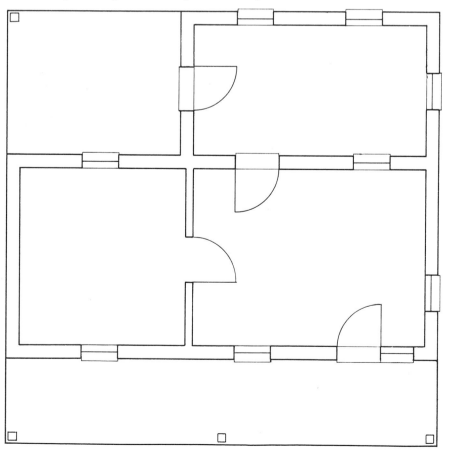

A two-and-a-half-story log house near Walnut Creek, Holmes County, Ohio. Now deserted and deteriorating.

End view of a log house now owned by Mr. and Mrs. James Hays. The exposed chinking between the logs will be covered with mortar.

108

An L-shaped farmhouse owned by Mr. and Mrs. Leroy Shoemaker, near Chillicothe, Ohio.

The Shoemaker farmhouse as shown in Gould's 1875 atlas of Ross County.

timbers were tenoned into the vertical ones. There were corner braces of considerable length, which provided rigidity to the structure. Channels were cut into the vertical members, and wide-split laths were fitted into the channels. One photograph shows hand-split laths of this type. The laths were then plastered on the inside and outside to form a wall that was smooth, nonconducting, and colorful. Sometimes the inside walls were whitewashed.

All of the half-timbered farmhouses seen by the author were at one time covered with clapboards, one still retaining most of its covering, another almost completely bare. The joinery and the plaster could not be seen, of course, if the weatherboarding were intact. The one with the joinery almost totally exposed demonstrates the amount of work required to build a house of this type. It has a porch, attached with rafters tenoned into a horizontal beam of the house structure.

Perhaps one of the most curious features of half-timber and log structures was that many were not equipped with fireplaces for heating and cooking. One log cabin examined had a fireplace in its basement, which probably served as a summer kitchen, for one side of it was on ground level. The lack

House of half-timber construction on the farm of Harvard Snyder, in Holmes County, Ohio.

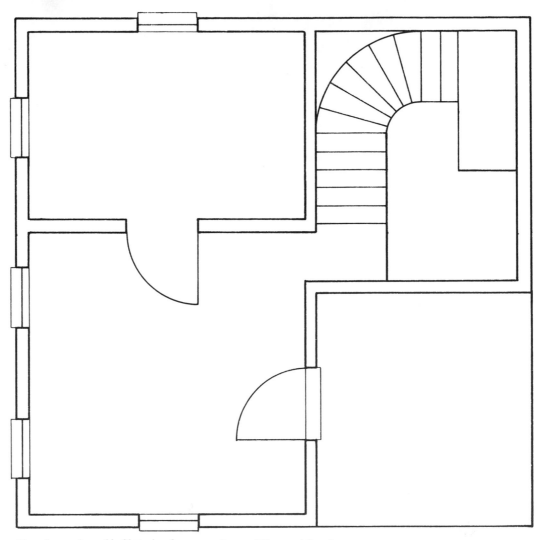

First-floor plan of half-timber house on farm of Harvard Snyder.

of fireplaces raises the question of how heating and cooking were accomplished in these otherwise primitive structures. The only answer seems to be stoves, which date from the middle of the nineteenth century, as do most of the houses, although ten-plate stoves were available in Pennsylvania early in the century. One example of a half-timbered house is the Brenly house, which was constructed in 1875 with timbers cut in a sawmill. Construction of the half-timber houses in Holmes County is attributed to the Amish, who emigrated from Germany and Switzerland.

An example of I-type construction can be found in a stone farmhouse near Bourneville, Ross County, Ohio. It is two rooms wide, separated by a hall, and one room deep. The second-floor arrangement originally was probably similar, but now one of the two rooms has a partition, thereby creating two rooms. The survival of the house in its original form can probably be attributed to the fact that it is located outside of populous areas. However, it

Joinery and laths of half-timber house.

will not be long until someone finds this structure for restoration and refurbishing.

The house is built of fieldstones and cut stones, the latter serving mostly as corners of the house. The huge and apparently original chimneys have survived, neither having had any masonry attention since the house was built. The window and door openings are unchanged. The number of windows is small, which suggests early construction and poor lighting. There are nine panes over six in all of the windows but one, the hall window on the second floor having six over nine. A portion of the outside wall was painted white, suggesting that at one time there was a porch, although it certainly was not an original appendage of the house. The house stands about a hundred yards from the road, and the porch was on the back side.

This farmhouse probably had its usual complement of outbuildings, of which one, a ground cellar, survives, located about twenty-five feet from the house. The surrounding terrain does not appear to be well-suited for farming, and it is doubtful that the farm was ever as large as a hundred acres. Also surviving in the backyard are two upright posts with forked limbs. On these were laid heavy timber for hanging butchered livestock.

The small size of this stone house (thirty by eighteen feet) suggests that such buildings soon became too small for growing families with associated farm activities. The problem of size was solved by a right-angled addition to the back of the house, usually forming a T or an L shape. The original back door served as an entry to the addition on the first floor, and a new staircase provided access to the second floor. The addition usually housed a large fireplace in its far gable end. There must be hundreds of farmhouses that evolved in this fashion. Life was more comfortable with the working area separated from the living area, and some continue to serve well as farm-houses today.

Small stone farmhouse of Clarence Smith, an example of I-type construction. Located near Bourneville, Ross County, Ohio.

If this evolving two-part farmhouse served the needs of the farmer well, the next step was obviously to build this kind of house from "scratch," and there is evidence that such a procedure was followed. Throughout the countryside one finds attractive farmhouses with front sections two rooms wide and one or two rooms deep, with an addition on the back. Many have fireplaces in the front rooms with a big kitchen-style fireplace in the back section, while some were found with one fireplace in the kitchen and none in the front. The absence of fireplaces suggests that the houses were built mid-century or later.

One of the most interesting farmhouses of this latter type is occupied by an Amish family at Winesburg, more or less the center of the Amish settlement in Ohio. The original sophistication of this house suggests that it was not built by the Amish but rather adapted to their needs. The original plan of the house was basically Georgian, with a center hall and stairs, and with two rooms on each side of the hall, on both the first and second floors. The

Farmhouse of Dr. and Mrs. William Garrett. This house was built in three steps.

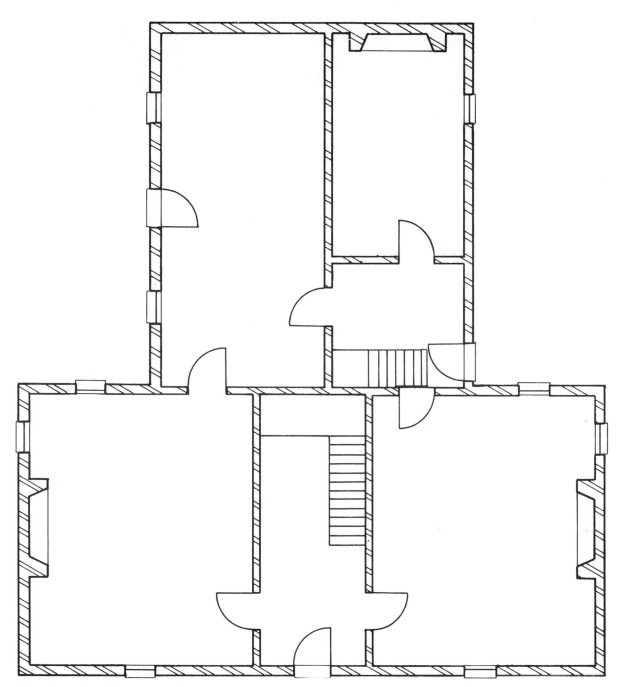

First-floor plan of the Garrett house.

Deserted Federal brick farmhouse, L-shaped, located near Chillicothe, Ohio, and owned by Mr. Alva McGraw.

partitions enclosing the hall have been removed, creating more useful living space as well as providing room for religious services.

There is a long extension on the back side, thus making it an L-shaped house. Most of the kitchen activity is centered here. The fireplace was situated in the basement of the back section, with easy access to the backyard. There big kettles of water could be heated, for washing and other kitchen chores. There is a large grape arbor near the house. In the backyard stands a smokehouse with a storage facility in one end. The enclosed front porch detracts from the architectural appearance of the house, but the one at the back probably remains unchanged from the time it was built. There is a fence around the garden, both survivals from earlier periods, with stone posts for the fence cleverly cut out to hold the horizontal members.

The Ohio farmhouses thus far discussed have been good substantial structures, well suited to the needs of farm life and the kind one would naturally expect to find in a community devoted to agriculture. Few have any outstanding ornamental features except for the house (owned by Dr. and Mrs. William Garrett) whose interior woodwork was made of walnut wood. As one travels over the countryside, one hopes to find a house or two that is an outstanding example of an architectural style, a slightly sophisticated house. Such a building is the Peter Wise house, located near Walnut Creek and built in 1841.

True to historical precedent, the builder of this house first lived for eight years in a log house on the site before building and occupying the present attractive structure. A move of this nature suggests that the owner, Peter Wise, had access to varied financial resources. He must have had substantial means when he came to the area, for he purchased a farm consisting of 700

Rear view of L-shaped farmhouse of Mr. and Mrs. Ivan Miller, near Winesburg, Ohio.

Stone fence posts around the Miller garden.

T-shaped farmhouse occupied by Mr. and Mrs. William Golden.

First-floor plan of the
William Golden farmhouse.

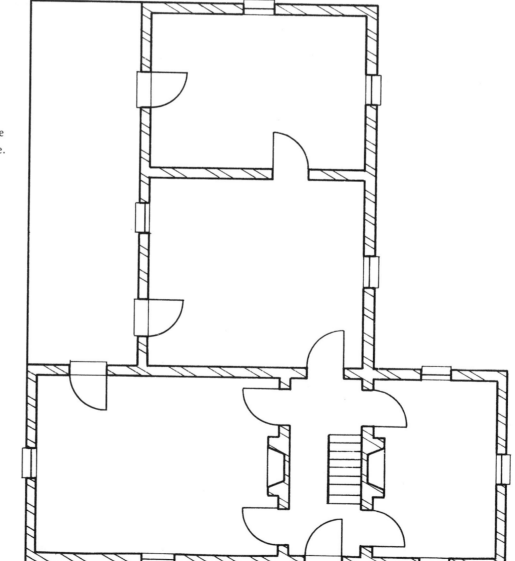

acres, an especially large farm for this area. Later, a small portion of his land was allotted for a school building, and it became known as Wise's School. It is known that Peter Wise was a miller, a trade that, combined with farming, may have substantially increased his wordly goods. In addition, there is evidence that the farm had a tenant house, another sign of affluence in this early period of settlement.

In some ways the house is conventional, but not for this area. The framework is covered with clapboards, and the foundation is of native sandstone. The stonework on the foundations of houses in this region tend to be of a very high quality, and this one is no exception. The floor plan is typically Georgian, with a center hall nine feet wide and a staircase leading to the second floor. All the rooms are essentially the same size, twelve by sixteen feet, with three windows in each room. The double-hung windows on the first floor have nine panes over six. The hall is well lighted by glass in the top portion of the door and attractive sidelights. When the author visited the house, sunlight was streaming through all the windows in the front of the house, giving the impression of warmth and light.

Another feature consistent with Georgian style is the presence of a paneled dado in the hall and in all the rooms on the first floor. The large plain surfaces of the dado and the doors suggest the influence of the Greek Revival period, but the colors of the original paint were of the eighteenth century. A recent Amish occupant of the house had all the woodwork grained in a muddy brown color. There were no closets in the house, clothing being unprotected on peg wardrobes attached to the walls. There was one closet in the kitchen to store culinary tools, which has been removed in recent years. There are folding doors between two bedrooms on the second floor, an arrangement designed to accommodate a large group of people for religious meetings.

The farmhouse had a variety of outbuildings at one time. There was an icehouse, which was supplied with ice from a nearby millpond. The summerhouse and its oven were destroyed years ago, and a later springhouse has replaced the one originally built on the site. There was a dryhouse, which was used to dry fruits and vegetables for use in the winter that has also been dismantled. The exact location of the privy is not known to the present owner.

The front porch is unquestionably part of the original structure, the floor and roof being framed when the house was built. The crossbeams of the floor are mortised into the front sill.

Although the balusters on the front porch have been replaced and some interior walls in the house have been restored to their original location, all in all, it is a remarkable farmhouse, and with care it will stand for another century or two.

Victorian farmhouses were built over a hundred years ago, when agricultural resources of the country were at their height. On the broad plain east of Columbus, the author visited a Victorian farmhouse, located near

The Peter Wise farmhouse, located near Walnut Creek, Ohio. Now owned by Stanley Kauffman.

First-floor plan of the Peter Wise farmhouse.

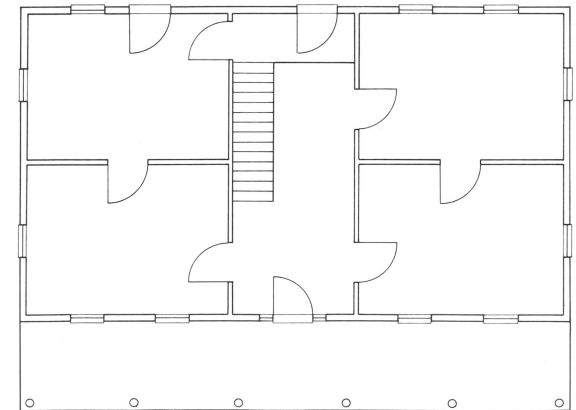

Lancaster, Ohio. The floor plan of this house is basically Georgian, the front part being one room deep and two rooms wide, with a hall and stairs between the rooms. It also has an appendage on the back, making the house a typical T shape. There is a fireplace in each of the front rooms, a custom from an earlier era.

The exterior of the house shares little with the Georgian style. The peak in the center of the roof introduces a new pattern that gives variety to an otherwise plain slanting roof. This variation has no effect on the interior arrangement of rooms. The roof extends considerably over the outside wall of the house, thus giving it some protection which it really doesn't need. The extension, however, does give the architect an opportunity to install large supporting Victorian brackets.

The cornice under the porch roof is ornamented with applied and cut-out designs, also typical of Victorian style. The front door has sidelights and a large transom, which gives considerable light to an otherwise dark hall. The lintels over the windows are typically Victorian, and the sashes have four panes each, instead of the earlier six or nine. This house is a very attractive example of Victorian architecture, and is owned today by Dr. J. L. Timmons.

Another Victorian farmhouse is located near Winesburg, Ohio. Although the exterior is only a modest example of the style, the interior arrangement of rooms shows a marked departure from earlier floor plans. There is virtually no hall, only a small landing inside the front door. The absence of a hall requires that one must pass through one or two rooms to get to a third room. In the front of the house are two rooms, one on each side of the stairs. Possibly one was a sitting room, the other a parlor. Across the back are three rooms, one being the kitchen, and the other two bedrooms. One of the back rooms may have served as a storage room, for there are obviously bedrooms on the second floor. There is no wasted space in this house.

The exterior view shows the roof extending over the outer wall, with a boxlike cornice supported by large brackets. The brackets and the overlay design on the frieze of the cornice establish the house as Victorian.

There are only a few windows, which are quite large, and have only two panes to a sash. The lintels over the windows are also ornamented in Victorian style. The house is the residence of Mr. and Mrs. Melvin J. Troyer.

In addition to the modest houses of working farmers, there were very elegant dwellings occupied by a breed of men known as "gentlemen farmers." The connotations of this occupation are not well-defined, but generally speaking, a gentleman farmer did not get his boots dirty on a regular daily schedule. He lived on the farm, and he occasionally went to the fields and the barn, but more or less only on an emergency basis. He probably helped at harvest time, when helping hands were at a premium, or performed any kind of work which could not be postponed indefinitely. He was usually wealthy, and his house and furnishings reflected his economic status. He may have been a land speculator, a government employee of some

Victorian farmhouse east of Columbus, Ohio. Courtesy of Dr. J. L. Timmons.

consequence, or a fortunate person who had inherited enough money to employ a tenant farmer who worked his land and cared for his livestock.

The houses of gentlemen farmers attract attention because a number have survived in reasonably good condition, or having been allowed to go to rack and ruin, they have been restored by philanthropists or historical societies. If restored by a government agency they are usually open to the public for a small admission charge. Although they are an interesting aspect of the farming picture, they cannot be regarded as "typical" farmhouses. There are three such examples in Ohio that are particularly interesting, including the Renick-Young house (private) near Circleville, the John Johnston farm at Piqua, and Adena, grand home of Thomas Worthington, an early governor of Ohio, near Chillicothe.

On the east side of the highway leading south from Columbus to Chillicothe, near Circleville, stands a fine house which would attract the eye of any farmhouse observer. This house, known as the Renick-Young house, is a low, rambling structure and was built in 1832. I. T. Frary points out that the house with its three corner bedrooms resembles Mulberry Castle, located

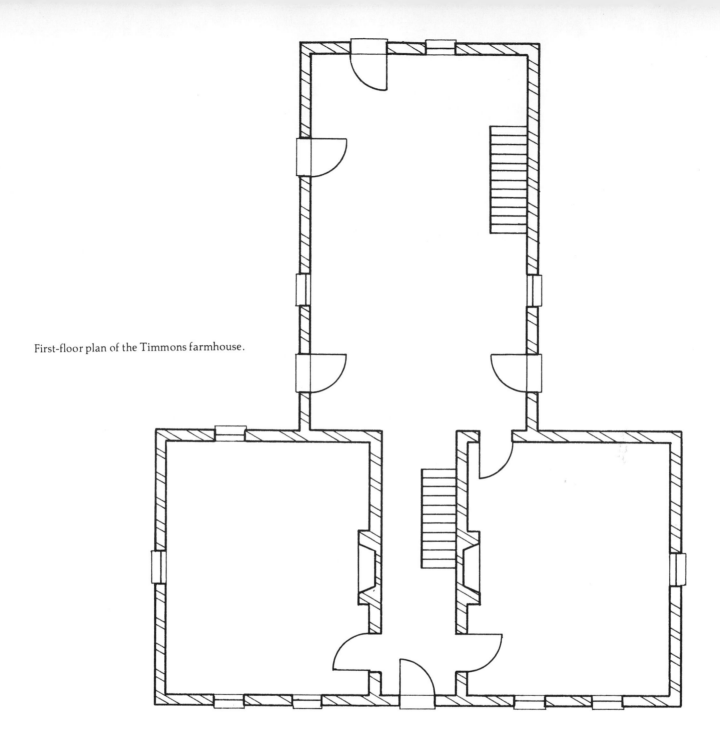

First-floor plan of the Timmons farmhouse.

in Goose Creek, South Carolina. The great distance between the two would suggest that the similarity is entirely coincidental. According to Frary the parents of William Renick, the builder, came from Hardy County, Virginia (later West Virginia). He later became famous as a cattle breeder and author and is credited with other important achievements.

Frary, while describing the house, points out that the central room is twenty-five feet square with a height of twelve feet. The design of the trim and the mantel indicate that the builder was a discriminating person and well aware of current styles. The Federal-styled mantel has a large cartouche in the center of the frieze and smaller ones at the ends.

Victorian farmhouse near Winesburg, Ohio. Courtesy of Mr. and Mrs. Melvin J. Troyer.

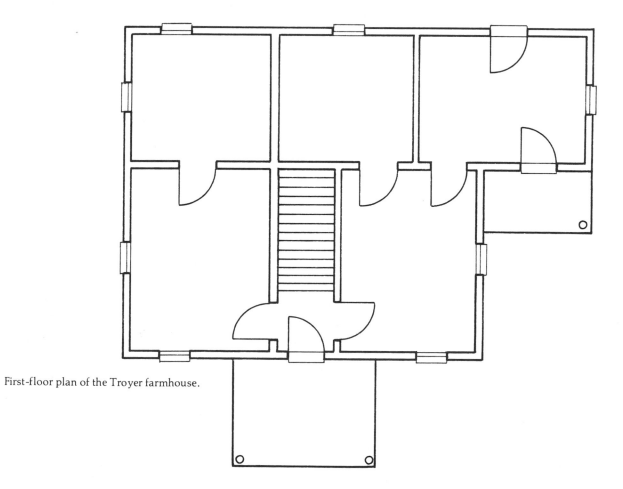

First-floor plan of the Troyer farmhouse.

124

Of the three corner bedrooms, one at the front right has no access to the rest of the house; the only entry to this room is off the porch. It probably was reserved for cattlemen, who were frequent guests. Renick was a nephew of Felix Renick, who introduced Shorthorn cattle to Ohio. The roof on the front portion of the house sweeps down over the porch, on top of which is a large dormer window, suggestive of a Southern influence, possibly Virginia. Instead of a bedroom at the rear left corner there is a dining room and an area possibly for servants.

About sixty miles west of Columbus lies the John Johnston farm at Piqua. Johnston was a very successful mediator in relations with Indians of the region. He was a man with broad interests, and his reconstructed house is a unique example of farmsteads built on the frontier in the early decades of the nineteenth century. A brochure published by the Ohio Historical Society describing the Johnston farm furnishes the following information. Johnston

John Johnston farmhouse built in 1815 at Piqua, Ohio. Courtesy of the Ohio Historical Society.

was born in Ireland in 1775, and by 1786 his family had emigrated to Carlisle, Pennsylvania. In 1802 he was appointed assistant factor for the government with the Indians at Fort Wayne. A few years later (1804–1805) he was able to buy 235 acres of land in the Piqua area, and by 1808 he had erected a log house and barn on the site and planted a large apple orchard. By 1810 his new brick house was started, but was not completed until 1815. During the war of 1812 he was again selected to reduce hostile Indian activity on the frontier, and he served as an agent until 1830. Throughout his life Johnston was concerned with national and community affairs. He was interested in canals and was a trustee of Miami University for twenty-five years.

The Johnston farmhouse, like many other farmhouses of the region was built in two sections. When completed the facade was basically Georgian, with a slight imbalance provided by two off-center attic windows. The imbalance of the interior, however, does not fit a Georgian pattern. There are three rooms of unequal size on the first floor, separated by two staircases, and flanked in the rear by a tier of balconies. The balconies are suggestive of an architectural influence from Virginia. A similar arrangement of balconies has been found in other parts of Ohio. In addition, the fireplaces are all located on outer walls, which was not a common procedure in Georgian architecture. The fanlight over the door and the sidelights suggest a Federal infleunce.

The fact that the house was built against a hill permitted the kitchen to be built in the cellar, with a ground-level access to the side yard. This feature is considered to be of Germanic origin and can be found in hundreds of homes in southeastern Pennsylvania. The heat and aroma of the kitchen were separated from the living quarters, but the food had to be carried up a flight of stairs to the dining room. This feature suggests the employment of servants, as well as a manner of life not commonly enjoyed by other farmers in Ohio.

Although existing records indicate later remodeling of the house, large areas of its recent history remain obscure. A sale bill appeared in a local newspaper in 1857 stating that the property was for sale and that the house consisted of fifteen rooms, all in an excellent state of repair. Near the end of the nineteenth century the house underwent considerable remodeling, only to fall into disrepair again, to the extent that the northeast wing was used as a sheep barn.

There is little about the house that indicates it was a farmhouse; however, the outbuildings which surrounded it suggest that an active ongoing farm was located there. An outstanding appendage was a log barn, consisting of two pens nearly thirty feet square and eighteen feet high. In 1826 a threshing floor was added, indicating that wheat, oats, or barley was one of the farm crops. The sale bill of the property appearing in a local newspaper stated that at that time the barn was 111 feet long and 54 feet in width. Adjacent buildings included a horse and cow stable, a cornhouse, a carriage house, a workshop, and a woodhouse. No mention is made of a facility for hogs, animals in which Johnston specialized, principally because they were not raised in large numbers by other farmers of the region.

A fruit kiln, commonly known as a dryhouse, stood on the property. There sliced fruit, such as apples and apricots, were placed in trays and slowly dried by means of a low fire. Two large apple orchards supplied fruit for eating and for making cider. There was also a cider house, where cider could be held at a fixed temperature to preserve it over a period of time. These two facilities have been reconstructed on the farm site.

The appurtenances most closely related to the house consisted of one large building, containing spring-, wash-, and smokehouses (illustrated in the section about springhouses). This building was also built against a hill, in this case permitting easy entry to the second floor from the ground level. The house was built over a strong spring, which discharged over ten gallons of water per minute, and which, in 1857, was conveyed to the house by a hydraulic ram. A tenant house, which was mentioned in the sale bill of 1857, also suggests that Johnston was a gentleman farmer. His other major interests must have taken much of his time; he certainly was not there to feed the cattle and milk the cows on a daily basis.

The house is open from ten to five, Tuesday through Saturday from April to October. Admission is charged.

Adena, the elegant farmstead of Thomas Worthington, is located near Chillicothe. Although this city is not particularly well known now, in Worthington's day it was the capital of Ohio and a very natural place for Worthington to live.

Thomas Worthington was born in Berkley County, Virginia (now Jefferson County, West Virginia), July 16, 1773. He was left an orphan at an early age, and when he was nineteen years old he set out on a two-year sea voyage aboard a British ship. In Glasgow he lost his money and had to return to America as a seaman.

In 1796 Worthington joined a party of men who set out to inspect the Virginia Military Tract between the Miami and Scioto rivers. At that time Chillicothe was a settlement of some twenty log houses. Worthington bought three lots and located warrants of General Drake (his guardian) in the same region. Worthington then returned to Virginia, and married Eleanor Swearingen. In company with others the newlyweds returned to Chillicothe in 1798, which by that time had grown to about a hundred houses. The immigrants built log houses, the unique one belonging to Worthington, which was described earlier. They brought with them valued personal possessions, livestock, and slaves. At the age of twenty-five Worthington was a man of property and had acquired considerable prestige in his newly adopted home territory.

The first legislature met at Chillicothe in 1803, when the state of Ohio was formed. Worthington was elected as one of the state's two senators, his term expiring in 1807. In 1811 he was returned to the Senate, and in December

Adena, the farmhouse of Gov. Thomas Worthington, located near Chillicothe, Ohio. Courtesy of Dard Hunter.

1814 he became governor of Ohio. The intervening years were spent on personal matters, one of the most notable being the building of Adena. In his diary he wrote, "Commenced laying of stone in the walls of my house with four masons."

The buff sandstone used for the house is a beautiful color, which seems to blend perfectly with its natural environment. The interior woodwork is composed of native walnut, while the floors are of ash and oak wood. Some of the flooring was quartersawed for resistance to the wear of many feet over the years. The brochure of the Ohio Historical Society mentions that Adena originally was called Prospect Hill, but in 1811 Worthington changed it to Adena, a Hebrew name that was given to "places for the delightfulness of their situations."

An architectural influence common in Virginia is easily discerned in the layout of the mansion. A raised courtyard is located in front of the main house, and flanked on each side by dependencies, both attached to the house. One is a kitchen facility; the other is now called a study, but may have originally served as Worthington's office. He was an avid land speculator, owned several mills, and was involved with other interests allied with farming.

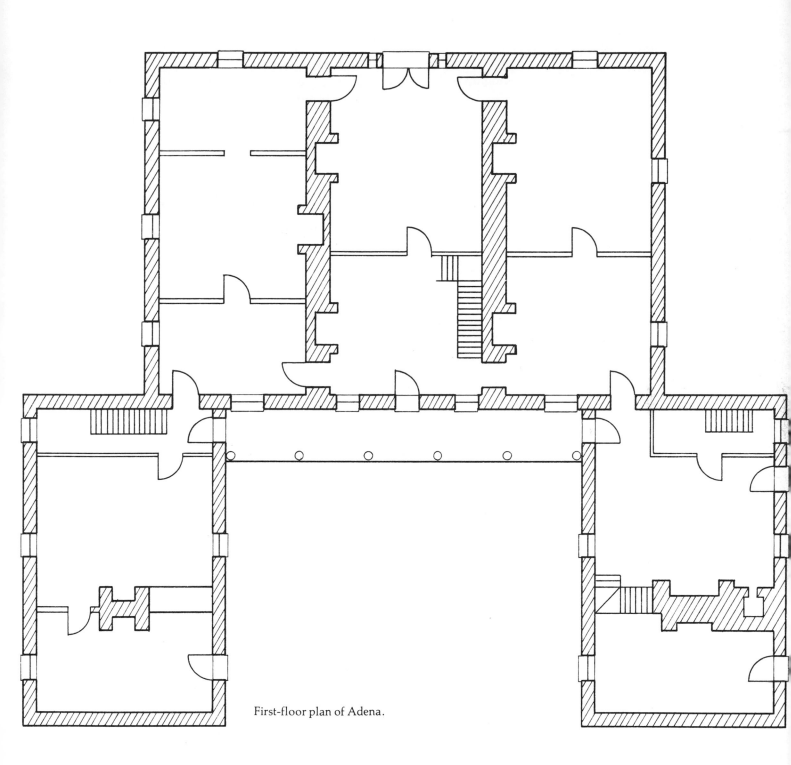

First-floor plan of Adena.

129

The kitchen has a bake oven built into a sidewall of the fireplace and is said to have held sixteen loaves of bread. There is a rotary spit for roasting meat before the fire, and a secondary spit with eight barbs for holding small fowl. There is also a worktable and chairs. In the adjoining pantry are found a demijohn, a sausage grinder, and an apple peeler. The location of these functional tools in the kitchen of the mansion attests to the fact that Adena was really a working farmhouse, as well as the residence of a gentleman.

Attached by only a roof to the main house is a washhouse sixteen by twenty-two feet, with a fireplace and a brick partition creating a storage room in the back. The roof is covered with lap shingles, the original ones probably being "double lap." Under the roof is a hand pump, which supplied water to the household.

West of the kitchen is a smokehouse, which was built during the same period as the main house. The transplanted Virginian probably relished ham and bacon in Ohio as he did in his earlier home. There are only a few small openings for the smoke to exit, and a door for easy access to the building.

A tenant house has been rebuilt on its original foundations. This house is conveniently located with easy access between the house and the barn. The barn has been rebuilt on its original foundations as well.

The main block of the house contains rooms now identified as a bedroom, hall, drawing room, and state dining room. Of lesser importance is a small parlor, an anteroom, and a family dining room. Also, a bedroom was located on the first floor, which was a common practice. All of these have fireplaces except the anteroom, which was probably heated by the fireplaces in the hall and the study. There are ten fireplaces within the house and its dependencies. It must have been a full-time job to keep all of the fireplaces operating at maximum strength.

There was a rotary serving shelf between the family and the state dining room, which permitted food to be brought into the state dining room without opening a door. A curious closet is located upstairs and was called a "crying closet." It has no windows, nor a knob on the inside for opening. Presumably, it was opened from the exterior when the crying stopped. There are six bedrooms on the second floor.

The house is beautifully furnished, with some of the furniture being made for the Worthingtons by local craftsmen. Other important pieces were made in New York, Pennsylvania, and Virginia. There is a tall case clock from Massachusetts. Fine portraits hang on the walls, and Oriental rugs cover the floors. There are interesting functional objects, such as knife boxes, a firescreen, and silverware, circa 1795 to 1830, that are mostly family pieces.

Part III
THE SOUTH

9 Virginia

Among the motives for colonizing in Virginia were a fanatic zeal to find gold and other precious metals, a source of supply for raw materials, and a mode of expanding the empire, in order to confront Spain, who claimed ownership of the Western Hemisphere. Farming was not one of the motives for colonization, and there is little evidence that the first houses in Virginia were built to be farmhouses.

An earlier attempt by the English to settle Roanoke Island in 1585 resulted in complete failure. The entire settlement was wiped out, and had the unfortunate victims been able to relate their experience to others who crossed the ocean, it is likely that subsequent attempts would have been more realistically executed.

None of the original settlers in Virginia were farmers. Obviously, this was a very critical weakness, and in later settlements, particularly Plymouth, virtually all the colonists were farmers, or descendants of farmers. The Virginians' lack of foresight in this matter is reflected in the list of tools recommended for the settlement, and reprinted in *Domestic Life in Virginia in the Seventeenth Century*, by Annie Lash Jester: "For a group of six men the following tools were deemed necessary: five broad axes, five broad hoes, five felling axes, four handsaws, a whipsaw, with filing equipment, two hammers, two hatchets, two frows, two handbills, a grind stone, nails of all sorts, and two pick axes." Although several of these tools might conceivably have been used for agricultural purposes, it is quite obvious that these tools were intended for building houses. This provision was not entirely foolhardy, for next to food, they did need shelter.

A lack of interest in farming is seen also by the site the colonists selected for settlement. They should have noticed that the land that they had chosen was either swampland or covered with dense forests.

From accounts of Virginia's first settlers in 1607, the triangular palisade, which they named James fort, looked like this hypothetical rendering of it. Inside the walls of the fort were simple homes for the 104 earliest settlers, as well as a church, guardhouse, and storehouse. Photo by Thomas L. Williams. Courtesy of the Jamestown Foundation.

Panoramic view of reconstructed farmhouses at Jamestown, Virginia. The first house on the right has a chicken yard enclosed with wattle.

Eventually the colonists of Virginia became farmers, but not before most had faced starvation, and the original plan of communal ownership of property was replaced by private ownership. Individual possession of land was of great importance to these colonists and it was a major reason for many coming to the New World. In England only an eldest son could inherit the property from his parents; the other men of the family could look only to continuous poverty and a life of hardship under a demanding landowner.

One of the first acts of the colonists in Jamestown was to erect a palisade around a prescribed plot of land and build houses within. The palisade was formed of timbers planted about four feet into the ground and extending ten feet above. The gates were opened during the day and closed at night. A supply of water as well as a storehouse were within the enclosure so that the colony could be sustained for a period if attacked by Indians. Eventually, sizable grants of land were made outside the enclosure, to which, when living was deemed safe, the families moved. In this way the colonists spread out, and towns were created.

There is not complete understanding of the houses that were built about the enclosure at Jamestown, but most historians agree that there was one room on the ground floor, a loft, and no cellar, a plan commonly followed by colonists at other sites. Cellars were bypassed at Jamestown because the water table was very high, and such a cavity would have quickly filled with water.

Actually, the structures built at Jamestown were similar to ones that the colonists had inhabited at home. A stout framework of hewed timbers was built, consisting of a sill on which studs and corner posts were mounted and topped with a plate, which held the rafters of the roof. One mode of making the outer wall was to entwine small branches between the studs and cover them with mud. This technique, which was also used in Plymouth Colony, was called wattle and daub. The mud withstood the mild Virginia weather for some time, but later it was found that a better method was to cover the framework with sawed or split planks. When this was done over wattle and daub, the house was well insulated. The planks were neatly placed horizontally around the framework, into which small openings were cut for a door and windows. The roof was covered with thatch, made of the abundantly growing marsh grass. Wooden chimneys of wattle and daub or split boarding were used. Although such chimneys were a terrific fire hazard, they were built well into the eighteenth century and finally were outlawed by local mandate.

The mild climate of Virginia would have permitted farmers to butcher animals, churn butter, or stew large quantities of meat outside the house. Domestic work, such as sewing, spinning thread, and molding cheese, could also be done outdoors; however, growing families along with improved financial circumstances lead to improvements in living quarters, both in size and in quality.

The common way for a Virginian to enlarge his house was to add another room lengthwise to the original one at the end opposite the fireplace. A fireplace was built in the addition, the result being a larger house with two fireplaces. This plan was later completed by erecting a partition crosswise in the second room, thus creating a corridor. The original room was called a hall, the second room a parlor. The house was sometimes expanded vertically; then the room over the hall became the hall chamber, and the one over the parlor, the parlor chamber. The two-room, two-story, all-brick house of Adam Thoroughgood is thought to have evolved in this manner.

The building technique of the settlement was slowly altered by the use of bricks. There was an adequate supply of clay in the region to make bricks, and archaeological excavations at the Jamestown site prove not only that there were brick foundations for a number of homes, but reveal the presence of kilns for hardening clay into bricks. One suspects that the first bricks produced were in short supply, available only for foundations and chimneys.

Another stimulus for making bricks was the dampness of the soil, which quickly rotted away the lower timbers of a house. The combination of bricks with a plank covering for the house made a satisfactory dwelling, and the surviving foundations attest to the fact that they were of lasting quality.

A few farmhouses were built along the Southeastern seacoast throughout the seventeenth century. After mid-seventeenth century, agricultural affairs gradually moved inland, and large plantation houses were built. In *Domestic Life in Virginia in The Seventeenth Century* by Annie Lash Jester, there is a report that in 1648 a man named Mathews built a manor house at the mouth of the Warwick River. Around the house was a miniature village where numerous activities flourished. Hemp and flax were grown, the flax being spun into yarn and woven into cloth, in one of the many outbuildings. Other workers included eight shoemakers, who worked in a tannery where leather was readied for them, and Negro slaves, some of whom worked with the crops, while others taught trades. Barley and wheat were raised in the fields, cattle grazed in the meadows, and swine and poultry wandered about the premises. Some cattle were kept for dairy purposes, while others were slaughtered and their meat sold to outgoing ships bound for the West Indies and Europe.

Thus, it becomes evident that, before the end of the seventeenth century, farming was pursued on a large scale. Attempts at founding towns in desirable locations were frustrated, and tidewater Virginia gradually became a vast area of self-sustaining plantations. In addition to the products mentioned above, Virginians found gold in the shape of a green leaf, called tobacco. The die was cast in favor of tobacco farming in Virginia until the present time, when tobacco was finally forsaken for the raising of grains and the grazing of cattle.

The earliest brick farmhouse to survive in Virginia was built by Adam Thoroughgood. Thoroughgood came to Virginia as a seventeen-year-old indentured servant in 1621. In three years he repaid the cost of his passage to America and soon thereafter acquired property. He returned to England, and after four years of residence there, he came back to America, bringing with him a wife and 500 settlers. For his contribution to the settlement of Virginia, he was awarded a Grand Patent of 5,350 acres of land along the Lynhaven River. The origin of this name can easily be traced to Lynn, England, where Thoroughgood was born.

Just how this former indentured servant built such a substantial house is still a mystery. One possibility is the income that he received from the sale of his vast acreage. Another possibility is the money he acquired by raising tobacco. Regardless of how Thoroughgood raised the money, he built in 1636 what is thought to be the oldest brick farmhouse in America. It has two rooms and a hall on the first floor and two rooms on the second floor. The fireplaces are located at the outer ends of the house, rather than in the center, as was the custom in New England. The window openings are small in the medieval manner, the small panes of glass being mounted in cames of lead, another English custom. When the house was restored, various architectural fashions of the eighteenth century were followed, particularly in the paneling around the fireplaces.

By moving inland from the seacoast of Virginia, one comes upon the farmhouses that are commonly known as plantation houses. These great houses lie along the James River, in the midst of thousands of acres. Certainly one of the finest of the great plantation farmhouses is Shirley, built before 1740 by John Carter. The present occupants and owners are descendants, the family of C. Hill Carter. The Carter family has been involved in local politics and business for many years. John Carter, the builder of Shirley, became Secretary of the Commonwealth for life in 1732. His family was associated with the construction of other outstanding buildings of this region, and his knowledge of architecture is attributed to his English schooling, plus whatever erudition he gleaned from architectural books after arriving in America.

The author visited Shirley on a dull gray morning and had the eerie feeling that he was about to visit an English manor house that had been transplanted to America. A "welcome" notice on the site stated that all the brick buildings had been built during the eighteenth century.

In front of the great house is a courtyard, referred to as a Queen Anne court. Immediately in the foreground are two angular buildings, which help to enclose the courtyard, on the left and right. At one time both of these served as storage facilities for farm products. Within the one on the right is a pit that served as an icehouse. The mild winter temperatures of the region make one curious about the source of the ice. In an excerpt from a Carter diary that was included in a study of Shirley by Catherine Lynn Frangiamore, there is mention of the year 1821: "Hardest winter since 1779–80, walked across the James river, and might have gone to Richmond." Another note about ice is found in the same source when activities of the

Exterior view of the brick farmhouse built by Adam Thoroughgood in 1636, located near Norfolk, Virginia. Courtesy of the Virginia Chamber of Commerce.

Interior view of the Adam Thoroughgood house showing the fireplace with an arched lintel, and paneling in the style of the eighteenth century. Courtesy of the Virginia Chamber of Commerce.

year 1830 are recorded. Among them is a February entry, "filling the ice house," and strangely enough there is another the same month, "Sowing clover seed." Not so strange is another, "hanging up bacon."

Between the two flanking buildings and the main house stand two 2-story buildings: The one to the left originally served as a laundry, while the one to the right served as a kitchen, but at present it is a place in which to buy gift items. In front of the court is a *dovecote*, which is a house for doves or pigeons that is usually raised at a height above the ground. It has internal provisions for roosting and breeding. Beyond and outside the court is a stable. Adjoining this is a smokehouse with a bell tower centered on the roof.

The exterior of the mansion is very impressive, particularly with its two-story porticoes with pedimental roofs. Both were built in 1831. They have a striking resemblance to a design by Andrea Palladio, and it is entirely possible that the resemblance is not purely coincidental. On both the

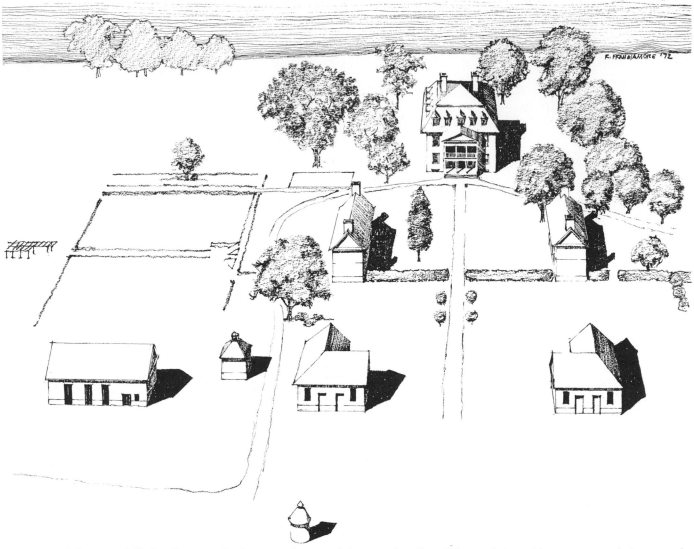

This aerial drawing of Shirley shows, in the foreground, a round dovecot, then (from left to right) a stable, a square smokehouse, and two one-story brick buildings which close off the forecourt that leads to the mansion. The L-shape buildings may have been used to store crops or supplies early in the eighteenth century. The one at the right incorporates an icehouse. Of the two matching buildings nearer the mansion the one on the left served as a laundry and schoolhouse in the nineteenth century; the one on the right is an eighteenth-century kitchen with living quarters. Beyond the mansion is the James River. Drawing by Roy Frangiamore. Courtesy of Catherine Lynn and Roy Frangiamore and the magazine *Antiques*.

Palladio design and the one at Shirley a baluster is found on the second floor but not on the first floor. The cornices of the porticoes and the house are ornamented with Wall of Troy dentils. Although the shape of the house is almost square, the porticoes seem to elongate it.

The floor plan of the house is unlike that of neighboring plantation houses, principally because it lacks a center hall. Instead of entering a hall, one immediately steps into a room that is both a hall and a main room of the house. The entrance is described by Frangiamore in an issue of the magazine *Antiques*, February 1973:

The entrance room is dominated by a spectacular walnut staircase that is familiar in its decorative details and general plan from English pattern books. The stairs rise from the first to the second floor in three sections, interrupted by two landings. The usual feature here is that from the second *landing to the second floor the flight of stairs* is not supported by any wall. The marvelous "flying" section is held up ingeniously by concealed L-shaped supports anchored to the wall. This construction secret was uncovered during recent repair work.

There is a slight discrepancy in this description, for the L-shaped angles are attached to an outer wall. What is missing is a second wall support, as found in most stairs.

The front room to the left of the entrance is furnished as a bedroom. Like many other farmhouses in various parts of the country, there was a practice of having a bedroom on the first floor. The second room on the river side of

View of first-floor bedroom of main house at Shirley Plantation. Photo by Haycox Panoramic, Inc. Courtesy of Shirley Plantation.

the house is the drawing room. It has a fine mantelpiece carved with oak leaves and acorns. One of the Carter children picked out some of the acorns, another from a later generation finished the job. In back of the hall is the dining room with brilliantly polished furniture and a crystal chandelier. The author particularly recalls a fine sterling sauceboat, with a skillfully turned handle of wood.

All the rooms are paneled from the floor to the ceiling. Among the decorative items gracing these panels is a rare pair of eighteenth-century hatchments or coats of arms. There are also many portraits of the various families.

The farm activity of Shirley plantation is recorded in four farm journals (1816–1872) that have survived and may be examined in the Library of Congress in Washington, D.C. A thorough study of these journals was made by Frangiamore, who subsequently described them in her manuscript entitled "Shirley Plantation Journals, A Survey." The contents of these journals cover a wide range of subjects. Among them one finds records of grains raised, sold, and consumed by the plantation (mostly wheat), farm practices which were, and were not, successful, the weather, financial accounts, repair of buildings, rotation of crops, shearing of sheep, application of soil conditioners, the welfare of slaves, directions for cutting timber, purchase of farm equipment, reclaiming of swamps, and personal notes concerning events such as marriages, all of which were important events in the business of running a farm. There are entries with reference to overseers employed at Shirley, many of their names being recorded. Curiously, there are no records of direct imports from Europe (there was a dock on the James River), and tobacco is mentioned only as a crop raised at Shirley before the records were kept.

In the journals, the problems concerning the raising and selling of crops seems to have priority over all other matters. An interesting entry is the one for June 13, 1824, about planting corn: "I find by experience that the best way to plant corn is 6 feet one way by 1½, one stalk, or by 3 feet, 2 stalks; that is to say, on good land & common corn, but hominy corn should be planted thicker and only on good land." Another entry, June 17, 1828, deals with cutting and shocking wheat: "Cutting and shocking wheat—dried up very much—and injured by rust; wheat ought to have been cut green and we ought to have saved more of it."

In lieu of earlier trade arrangements that Shirley might have had with English merchants, the major business transactions in the nineteenth century were with a firm in Richmond, Wortham and McGruder, and with others in Petersburg and in New York. For August 3, 1819, the following entry was made in a Shirley journal: "Went to New York with 1249 bushels of wheat and got a better price than the Richmond price." The grains were loaded on boats called "lighters," which docked at the Shirley wharf. An entry for February 18, 1823, states: "Finished delivering 100 barrels of corn to Neal Rices's lighter to send to Petersburg." In the same year 1,549 bushels of wheat were loaded on board a lighter destined for Petersburg.

Other important crops included clover and oats for the livestock. In the 1820s there was considerable experimentation with soil conditioners such as manure, marl, lime, and plaster. The fact that these were being used at Shirley suggests that modern methods of farming were being followed.

The size of the plantation was about one thousand acres, give or take about a hundred. There was constant buying, selling, and leasing of land, which made the size unstable for any great length of time. The visitor at Shirley today sees only the glow and glitter of rural family life in the eighteenth and nineteenth centuries, but reading the journals makes one aware of the realities of planning and perseverance. Shirley is located twenty-five miles east of Richmond and is open to the public every day except Christmas.

Moving northward in Virginia one comes to Loudoun County, where farming was pursued in a different way and by different types of people than those who worked and lived in the tidewater region. Although a few Cavalier English did settle where Leesburg and Middletown now stand, their efforts will be bypassed for other farms owned and operated by people with entirely different backgrounds. A stirring story is told of these people by Solange Strong Hertz in *Echoes of History*, vol. I, no. 2, a publication of the Pioneer America Society.

About 1725 the first emigrants, principally Quakers and smaller numbers of Baptists and Methodists from Pennsylvania, traveled south on what was later to be called the "Carolina Road." Many of the Quakers came from Bucks County, an area which they thought was inhabited by too many farmers at that time. Without slaves and without growing tobacco, these industrious farmers set up an economy based on farms, mills, meetinghouses, and crafts. Here, The Friends practiced liming, deep ploughing, and five-year rotation of crops. According to *Echoes of History*,

> These industrious peoples—Scotch, Irish, Germans, and Quakers—are largely responsible for the small thick-walled stone houses which abound in Loudoun County today. They were constructed from the very field stones turned up by the busy ploughshares of men who chopped their own wood, hauled their own water, and set barns and springhouses close to their dwellings. In the earliest houses, rooms are small, ceilings low, and stairs enclosed against drafts. Woodwork is simple and handmade, and doors are battened rather than paneled. There is always at least one cooking fireplace, and one huge chimney.

In this area, as in Pennsylvania, the first houses were built of logs. These structures served until land was brought under cultivation and the farmers' prosperity warranted new houses built of stone. One would expect that the new houses would have been more sophisticated residences than the log

The Hertz house near Leesburg, Virginia. Courtesy of Mrs. Solange Strong Hertz.

First-floor plan of the Hertz house.

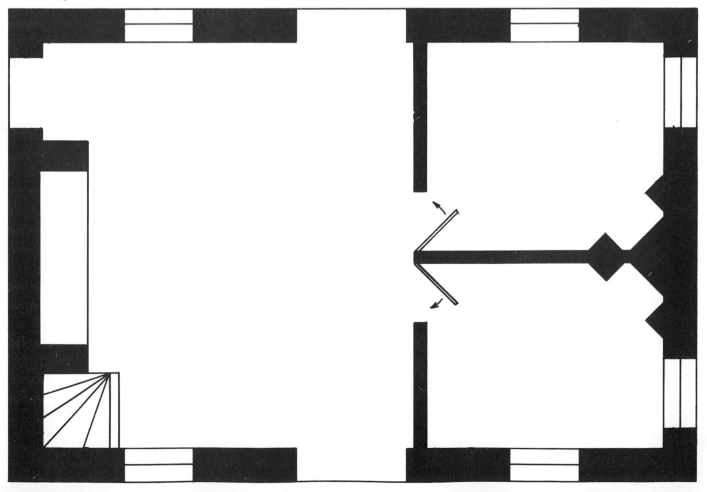

houses, but in many ways this was not true. They were more substantial, but not more extravagant.

The present residence of Mrs. Hertz has a Germanic floor plan with English locations of the chimneys. The first floor consists of three rooms, including a combination living room and kitchen with a large fireplace in the outside wall but not projecting beyond the outer wall. In one corner beside the fireplace a winding, narrow staircase leads to the second floor. There were two or possibly three windows in this room. There are two doors to the outside in opposite walls.

Adjoining the living room–kitchen and parallel to it are two smaller rooms, which served as bedrooms. Each of these has two windows and a corner fireplace. They are very pleasant rooms and were probably well heated. There is a board partition between the rooms on the first floor. The arrangement has been left untouched since the time that the house was built. There is a full basement under the house, it being a "bank house" with the entry to the basement on ground level. It is possible that, when this house was an active farmhouse, the basement was used as a summer kitchen. There is also a full second floor and a half attic. About fifty feet from the house a springhouse continues to supply water for the residence. This simple and charming house is a vestige of the past. Although it was never a mansion, it made a substantial home for a thrifty farmer.

All the farmhouses in Loudoun County were not small, snug houses like the one just described. Many were built at first on a small scale, but with increased prosperity they were made larger and more comfortable by additions of wings and ells. When these houses fall into the hands of resourceful owners today, they are restored to a degree of elegance, sometimes exceeding the original, with the grounds beautifully landscaped and stone walls, boxwoods, and brick walls added.

An example of a larger house is one known as the Minor Bartlow house, his name being inscribed on one of the lintels found in the house. The house was first occupied by the family of Jacob Janney, who was born in Bucks County, Pennsylvania, in 1704. The following information is provided in the booklet "The Minor Bartlow House," by Elizabeth and John Lewis, the present owners and occupants of the house:

> Having sent a request for a warrant and survey in 1741, Jacob Janney purchased from the office of the proprietor of the Northern Neck of Virginia, "honourable Thomas Lord Fairfax, Baron of Cameron, in that part of Great Britain called Scotland, proprietor of the Northern Neck of Virginia," a grant of 270 acres in 1744.

Sometime thereafter a house was built on the site. A hypothetical floor plan, as drawn by John Lewis, suggests that the first house consisted of only two rooms, a kitchen and a parlor, the parlor doing double duty as a bedroom. There was a fireplace in each of these rooms, and in the kitchen a staircase led to the second floor, which contained two or three bedrooms. A stoop provided entrance to the kitchen on one side, and opposite was another door.

Blackstone Janney, the eldest son of Jacob and Hannah, was born in 1741 and married Mary Jane Nichols in 1763. They had eight children between the years 1770 and 1785. Blackstone inherited or bought the property and subsequently enlarged it during his occupancy. He added a new kitchen wing in line with the original two rooms, and running along one side was a cold-storage room. The new kitchen wing contained a fireplace and a staircase leading to the second floor. There was a separate entry to this kitchen, and, of course, a door was cut through to connect it with the earlier portion of the house. The stairs from the kitchen led to a second-floor bedroom and was the only means of access, there being no connecting door to the rest of the house. This arrangement suggests that the bedroom was used primarily by a servant or other hired help.

Blackstone Janney had a son Eli, who eventually purchased the Minor Bartlow house, along with eighty-nine acres. John Lewis has projected that between 1815 and 1825 another kitchen was added in line with the other rooms. It, too, was provided with a separate entry and a staircase leading to

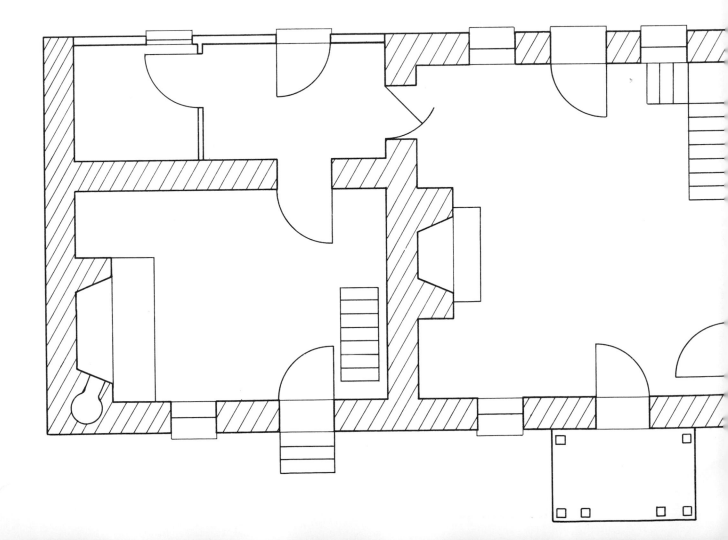

The restored Minor Bartlow farmhouse of Mr. and Mrs. John G. Lewis, near Hamilton, Virginia.

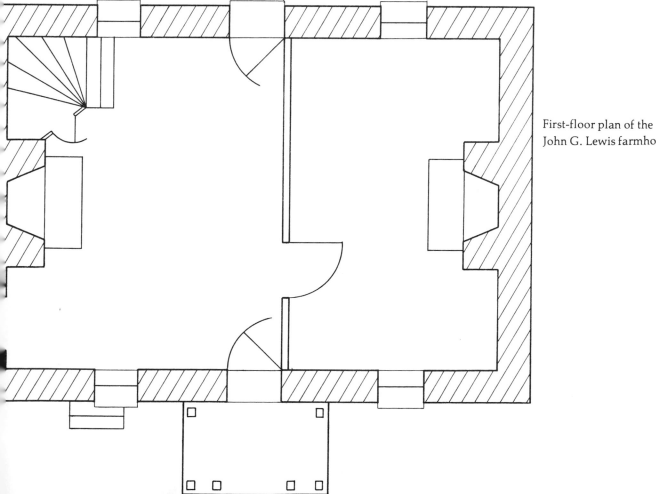

First-floor plan of the
John G. Lewis farmhouse.

147

the second floor, as well as a large cooking fireplace. The earlier kitchen was converted to a dining room; the other two rooms became a hall and a parlor. There were now three outside entries along the front of the house, and three in the rear. Another outside entry led to the cellar in the oldest section of the house, a convenience found in many farmhouses for the easy storage of food raised in the vegetable garden. The photograph of the house as it appears today shows how a sophisticated dwelling can be created from a very functional farmhouse. The Janneys were undoubtedly frugal, hardworking farmers.

Originally, there was a complement of outbuildings on the property, including a springhouse, smokehouse, and barn. The smokehouse has survived intact. It is unique in the fact that the fire could be stoked from the outside, thus eliminating the necessity for the farmer to enter a smoke-filled room. The spring has been enclosed by a modern structure.

In Louisa County, about twenty miles east of Charlottesville, a section of area is known as "Green Springs." It has a unique assemblage of rural architecture, preserved very much as it was about two hundred years ago. In recent years the owners of these properties have banded together to fight legal battles to maintain their virtually untouched rural landscape. In the application to become a National Historic Landmark (a status that was finally achieved), the community was described:

> For a century, perhaps for two, the landscape, the rural mode of life and the blend of the buildings in their setting has remained substantially undisturbed. Even fence lines and meandering country lanes, mostly unpaved, follow their original course. In fact, descendants of original families still hold land in several instances. While only several historic buildings might qualify as exceptional, the ensemble amounts to a product much greater than its parts. Notable are the unusually large number of surviving outbuildings, a fact attributable the the continuous vitality of both the soil and the community. The most outstanding of the manors have from seven to twenty historic outbuildings—smokehouses, kitchens, icehouses, barns, slave quarters, schools, offices, carriage houses, barns, spinning houses and more.

It is pointed out that samples of architecture from the Colonial era until just after the Civil War survive there. Their very names suggest historical relevance or are descriptive of natural features. Among them are "Peers House," "Corduroy," "Grassdale," "Galway," and "Hard Bargain."

One would naturally expect to find the soil of the area very rich and productive. Travelers mentioned it in their journals and the *Gazeteer of Virginia* observed that Green Springs "far exceeds all the high land in the county, both in native fertility and in susceptibility of improvement." It was

PLATE 1.

Painting of Bronck farmstead at Coxsackie, New York, by Richard W. Hubbard, c. 1870. To the left is an early Dutch barn, and a unique thirteen-sided barn, not shown in the painting, is located beyond the lower right corner of the pasture. *Courtesy of Bronck House, Coxsackie, New York.*

PLATE 2.

Farmhouse of Mr. and Mrs. Sperry Morway at Glastonbury, Connecticut. The rear section of this house was built in 1687, and the front section was added in 1716. Its unusual features include a gambrel roof and a "coffin door," which is located on the side near the front wall.

PLATE 3.

Farmhouse of Mr. and Mrs. Sherman Carpenter of Kensington, Connecticut. This house originally was built in 1786 as a small one-and-a-half story house. It was enlarged in 1838.

PLATE 4.

This stunning Victorian farmhouse was built in 1861. The house is owned by
Mr. and Mrs. Frank Kimball of Kensington, Connecticut.

PLATE 5.

The Christian Herr House, near Lancaster, Pennsylvania, was completed in 1719. The owner carved his initials and the date into the sandstone lintel of the front door. One of the oldest farmhouses in Pennsylvania, it is built of field stone, and the architecture is Germanic.

PLATE 6.

The Jacob Martin farmhouse was built by Johannes and Anna Hersche in 1805, although the style of the house, English Georgian, precedes this date by twenty-five years. The farmstead is located in Manor Township of Lancaster County, Pennsylvania.

PLATE 7.

Very little is known about the origins of the Kendig dairy house near Millersville, Pennsylvania. One unusual feature is the presence of two front doors.

PLATE 8.

The David Mayer farmhouse is a Victorian structure with an unusually large front porch and an attractive cupola on the roof. It was built in 1867 and is located on the Fruitville Pike near Lancaster, Pennsylvania.

PLATE 9.

This deserted two-and-a-half-story log house and summer house is located near Walnut Creek, Holmes County, Ohio.

PLATE 10.

A deserted half-timber or *fachwerk* house, probably built in the first half of the nineteenth century. Holmes County, Ohio.

PLATE 11.

Reconstructed log buildings at Schoenbrunn, Ohio. The original cabins on the site were built in 1772.

PLATE 12.

Shirley Plantation House in Charles City County, Virginia, was built prior to 1740 by John Carter. The impressive two-story porticos with pedimental roofs were added in 1831. *Photograph courtesy of The Jamestown Foundation.*

PLATE 13.

This deserted overseer's house in Hertford County, North Carolina, was built about a hundred years ago. It has several unique features, including "clay pots" for chimney caps, unusual posts with corner brackets on both of the front and back porches, and an attractive frontal peak in the roof.

PLATE 14.

The Griffin farmhouse near Pine Top, North Carolina, has an attractive facade with an unusual second-floor porch. The farmstead consists of about five hundred acres, and the house was built about one hundred years ago.

PLATE 15.

The Clark farmhouse, near Gainesville, Georgia, was built during the nineteenth century.

PLATE 16.

An attractive pump and pump cover on the Clark farmstead.

PLATE 17.

This deserted log cabin, located near Gainesville, Georgia, has been covered over with clapboards. Originally a one-room structure, it now consists of two rooms. The lovely red color of the bricks in the chimney contrasts well with the rich brown of the clapboards.

PLATE 18.

The Hardman farmhouse in White County, Georgia, was built in 1870 by James H. Nichols. It is a grand example of Victorian architecture.

PLATE 19.

The springhouse on the Hardman farmstead was built in the style of the mainhouse.

PLATE 20.

The lovely barn on the Hardman farmstead is large and commodious. It, too, was built in 1870.

PLATE 21.

This charming springhouse near Rawlinsville, Pennsylvania, has a bake oven attached to the rear (*left*) and an outside entrance to a root cellar.

PLATE 22.

The weathered boards in this frame summerhouse have turned a lovely color, and the bell tower on the roof is particularly charming. Near York, Pennsylvania.

The front view of the Iona farmhouse built in 1770 by Maj. James Watson at Trevilians, Virginia. Courtesy of Mrs. Hiram Ely.

Plot plan of Iona showing the location of various farm buildings. Courtesy of the Green Springs Historic District.

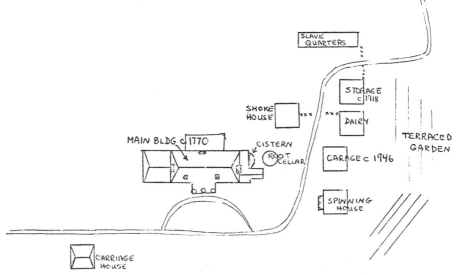

"particularly suited to wheat, yielding 8 bushels of seed, without manure, and capable of being made to yield 15, 20 or 30 to one." Green Springs, like other regions of Virginia, grew large stands of wheat, some of which was ground into flour in the local gristmills. Gradually, wheat growing declined in favor of stock raising, which is the dominant activity of the farms today.

Green Springs is represented in this survey by two farms, Iona and Hawkwood. Iona is a charming house, originally a two-room, one-and-a-half-story structure with end chimneys. This plan was encountered in houses built earlier in the tidewater area, and it must have proved satisfactory for the occupants. Like other houses, Iona grew. Additions were made on the north, east, and west, although little change was made to the original structure. Among the remaining buildings are a carriage house, a dairy, a smokehouse, slave quarters, and a frame barn. The barn is reputed to be the oldest "documented timber barn in Virginia . . . and an exceptional example of early timbering techniques in Piedmont, Virginia."

Iona was built in 1770 by Maj. James Watson. The present owners, the Hanger family, told the writer that Major Watson was so successful in growing wheat that he was called "Shocker" Watson. The accompanying line drawing shows the location of different buildings on the site. It was taken from the manuscript "Green Springs Historic District, An Application to become a Registered National Historic Landmark."

Hawkwood is another important farmhouse in Green Springs. It is a Tuscan-styled villa, designed by Alexander J. Davis, and built from 1852 to 1854 by Richard O. Morris, a descendant of an early settler in the Green Springs area. According to "Green Springs Historic District,"

> Hawkwood is one of the most important romantic country houses in America. It is the finest and best preserved surviving Tuscan villa of A. J. Davis, who is widely regarded as the outstanding American designer of country houses in his period. He was especially noted for his houses in romantic picturesque styles, designed to be in harmony with rural landscape settings. . . .
>
> Hawkwood is one of Davis' masterpieces. It was designed at the height of his interest in the Tuscan style, shows his great skill in handling irregular composition, and embodies features characteristic of his designing. Its arcaded veranda is notable and is unique among the surviving Davis villas.

This lovely homesite is located at a distance from the road on a knoll that affords sweeping views of surrounding countryside. The interior of the house is virtually unchanged from the time it was built. One enters the house through an arcade leading into a hall. On one side of the hall the drawing room is located, on the other side, a chamber. Continuing straight through the hall one enters a dining room flanked on the left by stairs leading to the

Water color rendering by A. J. Davis of Hawkwood, built for Richard O. Morris in Charlottesville, Virginia. Courtesy of the Metropolitan Museum of Art, Harris Brisbane Dick Fund,
1924.

First-floor plan of Morris House. Courtesy of the Metropolitan Museum of Art,
Harris Brisbane Dick Fund, 1924.

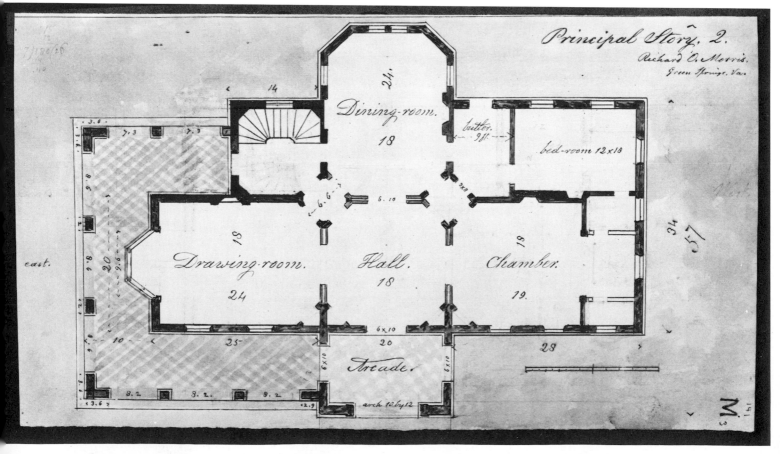

second floor, on the right by a bedroom. The ample rooms have a ceiling height of fifteen and a half feet. The exterior is attractively landscaped with a number of large boxwood bushes and other evergreens.

A number of scattered outbuildings have survived, including three barns, servant quarters, a smokehouse, a privy, a log house, and the house originally built on the site. These add variety and interest to the setting.

The owners are Col. and Mrs. Hiram Ely, Mrs. Ely being one of the most persistent, among others, to have the area recognized as an Historic District. The house is not open to the public. However, on certain days when the public is invited to visit specified houses in the area, some of these houses are included in the tour.

The last in this survey of farmhouses in Virginia is located near Middletown. This attractive house was built of brick at about the time of the

Small eighteenth-century farmhouse at Mangohick, Virginia. Note that there are living quarters on the ground floor. Courtesy of Mr. and Mrs. Sterling C. Louthan.

Brick farmhouse with Georgian characteristics built at the time of the Civil War. Residence of Mr. and Mrs. John Whitman, near Middletown, Virginia.

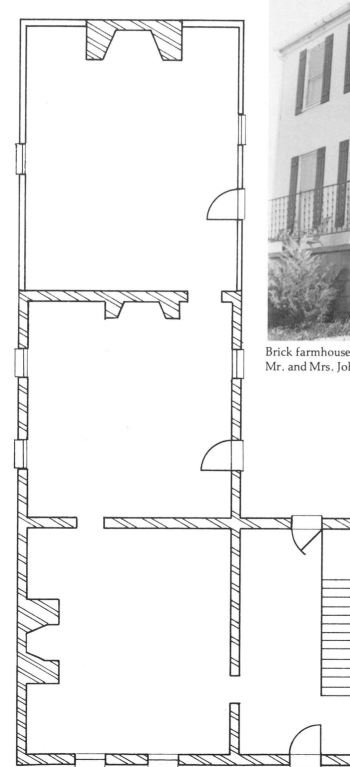

First-floor plan of the Whitman residence.

153

Civil War. The floor plan shows that it was a simple house, with traces here and there of elegance. Architecturally, it is known as a half-house, that is half of a full Georgian house, and it has some Georgian characteristics. There is a spacious hall with stairs leading to the second floor. The other first-floor rooms include a living room and what was originally a working kitchen–dining room with a fireplace. In addition a summer kitchen with a fireplace is attached to the house. It was used for cooking, baking, and such farm work throughout the year that was unsuitable for the main kitchen. The Federal doorway has a Georgian broken pediment at its top.

This farmhouse is located on a site of 130 acres, reduced from its original size of 200 acres. Only a barn remains of the outbuildings, and its primary uses were to shelter animals and to store the products of the fields. The principal crops were corn, wheat, and hay.

Although the popular image of rural Virginia is one of rich soil, nourishing field after field of tobacco, this concept was approximated mostly in the river basins of the James, the York, and the Rappahannock rivers. The soil of the river valleys of Virginia now produces cereal grains. In 1868 the major crops of the state were Indian corn and wheat, followed by rye and oats, barley, buckwheat, potatoes, tobacco, and hay, with barley and buckwheat being raised in the smallest quantities. Among the livestock were horses, mules, oxen, milk cows, sheep, and hogs. In the same year Virginia produced 160,000 bales of cotton and shipped out annually 15,000,000 bushels of oysters.

In farmhouse architecture the great plantation houses of Virginia are unique in America, possibly in the world. The economy which produced them was shaped by the rich productive soil.

10 North Carolina

In North Carolina, the first settlement was made in the northeastern part of the state by emigrants from Virginia. There is no evidence, however, of any farming activity dating from the seventeenth century, and only a few buildings of the eighteenth century have survived. One would expect to find farm buildings from the eighteenth century in the central piedmont section of the state, which was settled principally by Pennsylvanians with agrarian interests, many of whom were Moravians from Bethlehem. Actually, the early holdings, which were often as large as 500 acres, can hardly be identified now.

The situation is different in the northeastern part of the state, where a relatively large number of farms of the nineteenth century are still in use, some having remained in the possession of one family for generations. This area is essentially rural with no large metropolises, and consequently land holdings have remained large, many to the extent of several hundred acres.

The first settlements of North Carolina were made in Hertford County. The urban center of Hertford County is Murfreesboro, a small city which is enjoying a renaissance by adapting old structures to modern uses. Around the city lie vast acres of rich agricultural land, probably as productive now as it has been in the past. Although modern farming equipment is used everywhere, a striking number of farmhouses have survived with little or no changes.

Visits to a number of properties leads one to suspect that the pattern of farmhouse building in North Carolina was similar to that of Virginia, but on a more modest scale. Although there are plantation houses, none is comparable in size or style to Carter's Grove, Westover, or Shirley. A number of overseers' houses have also survived, as well as unpretentious ones in which field workers lived. A few of these houses have been kept in top-notch condition, others are shabby and neglected.

Mid-nineteenth-century farmhouse and office, now deserted, on the Princeton farm, near Murfreesboro, North Carolina.

House presently occupied by an overseer on the Princeton farm.

The first property visited by the author was a house and separate office at Princeton Farm in Northampton County, which was occupied previously by an overseer, but is now left to the weathering effects of the elements. (The farm in now the property of Mrs. Cecil M. Forehand of Murfreesboro.) The house was probably built about the middle of the nineteenth century, with a simple floor plan of two rooms in the front and a kitchen in the rear. The two front rooms have chimneys, indicating the presence of fireplaces; the rear kitchen, having none, was probably a later addition and equipped with a stove.

There is little evidence that the house was geared to farm life, although it now stands in the middle of a large field. Under the center of the front portion a brick cellarlike enclosure was built to provide cold-storage room for root crops and possibly fruit. There is no entrance to this enclosure from within the house, perhaps because it was constructed at a later date. This house, like many others in the region, has never had a traditional cellar; the high water table of the area would have led to frequent flooding. Part of the porch on the back of the house has been enclosed to provide a dry-storage area. The roof is covered by sturdy sheet metal, but the unpainted clapboards will eventually deteriorate, and the house will be razed.

Near the house stands an old office of the overseer, where accounts were kept and other plantation business transacted. The presence of a chimney

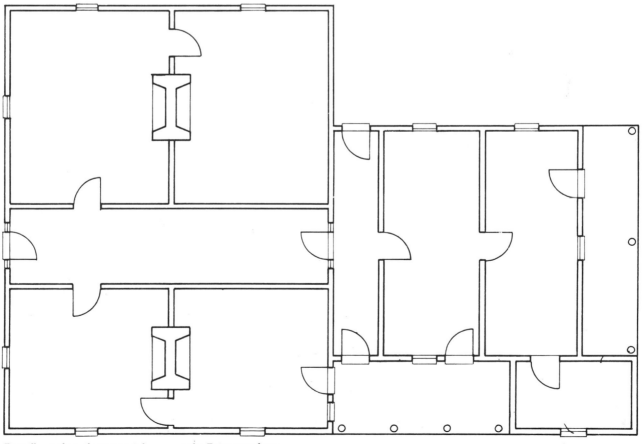

First-floor plan of overseer's house on the Princeton farm.

Deserted overseer's house with Victorian characteristics in Hertford County, North Carolina.

and a fireplace suggest that the building was frequently used, and probably over long periods of time.

About five or six hundred feet from the old overseer's house stands a more modern building, which is inhabited today and in a good state of repair. This house, like the one just described, is elevated off the ground about eighteen inches, in order to protect the house and its occupants from the damp ground. The main area of this house consists of two pairs of rooms, separated by a spacious hall. This feature, as well as the ornamented doorways, suggest the house was intended to be more than just a satisfactory dwelling. The unusual feature of these rooms, however, is the presence of a fireplace in each of the four. The fireplaces were built into the partitions between the rooms. It appears that these four rooms constituted a complete house at one time, for the doorway at the rear of the hall is equally as attractive as the one in front. There are side windows on each of the doorways.

To the rear wall of the house an appendage with a fireplace was attached. This one was intended for cooking and other household work. Originally a porch was built along one side of this rear addition. One part of it has been converted to a bathroom, the other end to a storage closet. The rooms are heated today with a modern space heater.

Several miles away stands another overseer's house with a floor plan of the main portion that is similar to that of the main house on the Princeton farm. This house has an addition attached to the rear at an end instead of in

158

Overseer's house in Hertford County, built about 1830, exhibits Greek Revival elements. Courtesy of Cecil Maddrey.

the center, so that it forms an L rather than a T. Since it was built about a hundred years ago, it contains Victorian elements. The chimney caps are "clay pots," which seem to be unique to this house, although the writer, not having examined a great many houses in the area, cannot vouch for this with certainty. Instead of the usual sloping roof, a peak appendage on the front adds variety and makes the roof line attractive. The posts on the front and back porches have corner brackets. This house in its heyday met more than the minimum requirements for a dwelling, but it is now well on its way to rack and ruin.

Another overseer's house in the same countryside exhibits a few qualities of Greek Revival architecture, having been built about 1830. It has a central hall, as do many houses of the region, with fireplaces in the rooms on each side of the hall. The full-length pillars on the porch give the front of the house the appearance of a small temple. This charming house is being cared for, as evidenced by fresh paint and substantial shutters all around the house. The present owner is Mr. Cecil Maddrey of Severn, North Carolina.

In some ways the most impressive house is one located on Bynum Plantation, which was built in 1842. (Now owned by Cyrus D. Howell, it is located in Maneys Neck Township in ertford County.) It sits back from the road near the center of the grounds. It consists of a front block of rooms, two stories high, with porch columns reaching from the first floor to the roof. The round columns are fluted from top to bottom, and give the house an appearance of dignity. A center hall on the first floor is flanked by one room on each side,

House on the Bynum plantation in Hertford County, built in 1842, with porch columns that reach from the first floor to the roof.

each having a fireplace. The mantels are very simply designed. The windows on the first floor are quite large, eliminating the necessity for two windows in order to achieve adequate light, with shutters designed to cover only the sidelights of the windows. There is an entry into the cellar on each side of the house leading to separate compartments, with one room between them. It is believed that one room was reserved for male slaves, the other for female slaves. The center one, which resembles a dungeon, was used to incarcerate slaves for discipline measures.

An original separate kitchen stands at the rear of the house, obviously designed to keep the aroma and heat of the kitchen out of the main house. This is a spacious room, and it has a very large fireplace. It is now attached to the main house by another room that serves as a dining room. Many years ago two lines of crepe myrtles formed the boundaries of the walk toward the entrance of the house.

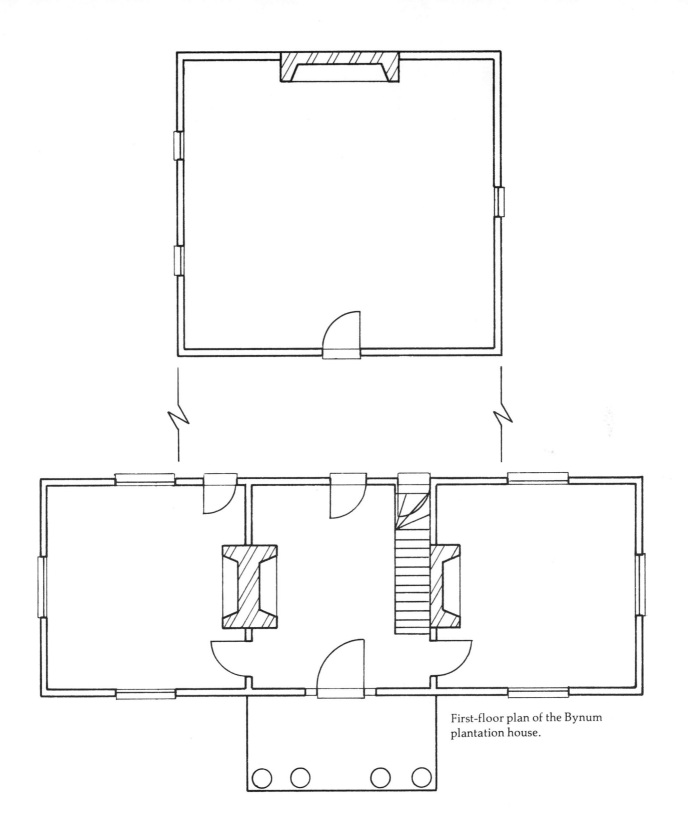

First-floor plan of the Bynum
plantation house.

Deserted servants quarters on the Bynum plantation.

Another important farmhouse in Hertford County is the Hare plantation house (owned by Mrs. Joyce Sumner), which was built during the last quarter of the eighteenth century. The facade is very attractive with a balanced arrangement of windows, each one having nine over nine panes. The paneled door has a transom to allow a bit of light; however, the entry room-hall is well lighted by three additional windows. The clapboards have a beaded edge and are of a fine quality.

In some ways Hare House, located three miles west of Como, North Carolina, seems like a smaller replica of Shirley Plantation in Charles City County, Virginia. The portico is only one story high, while the one at Shirley is two stories. The portico lacks the dentil molding, but the cornice of the main house has a very attractive example of a dentil molding. The room layout on the first floor is also reminiscent of Shirley's. Through the front door one immediately steps into a large room instead of a hall. As a matter of fact, this room serves as a hall. A set of stairs is located against one of the outside walls, in a manner similar to the arrangement at Shirley, although this is not an example of the flying type, since it is supported on both sides.

Oddly enough, there are no fireplaces in the two front rooms. In the back rooms the fireplaces are of normal size, but above them is built a large ornamented chimney piece that reaches almost to the ceiling. These fireplaces have massive chimneys, built entirely outside the house, a traditional procedure in this part of the country. Although this is a tenant house now, it is apparent that in its day it stood out in the community.

Hare house on the Hare plantation in Hertford County, North Carolina. Once a plantation.
house, it now serves as a tenant house.

First-floor plan of Hare house.

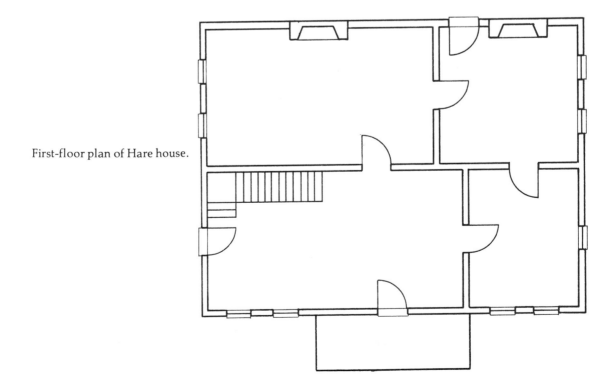

The Roberts-Vaughan house in North Carolina has been restored. It is situated with its outbuildings on the main street of Murfreesboro. A pamphlet describing the house tells that it was restored for use as a public library with offices for the chamber of commerce, the Murfreesboro Historical Association, and the Industrial Development of the region. It also includes a children's reading room, public meeting rooms, and an information center. The remaining 1.3 acres of land will be developed into a public park. The adaptive use of this fine old house has created nationwide interest in such a project, and it is highly likely that other communities will follow a similar procedure. The brochure further states:

> We do not think we are stretching a point when we say that the site is a rare one indeed. It is most unusual in this advanced technology that we live in to find a beautiful 18th century site intact in the heart of a central business district. With its original plantings of crepe myrtle, cedar and oaks, the Roberts (Vaughan) site has withstood the march of time and today is one of the most beautiful sites in America.

The house was erected in two parts, the first in the late eighteenth century, around 1790, when the Jonathan and Benjamin Roberts families of North-Hampton County, North Carolina, built the original section. The original section is the left side as one faces the front. Around 1835 the property was owned and enlarged by Col. Uriah Vaughan. It remained in the possession of the Vaughan family until it was bought by the Murfreesboro Historical Association and deeded to the City of Murfreesboro for restoration.

A thorough check of the building was made, and although the exterior showed some evidence of disrepair, the interior walls and floor were found to be virtually intact and sound. The foundation of English-bond bricks was firm and solid, as were the sixteen-by-sixteen-foot sleepers and the six-by-sixteen-foot floor joists. All were made of North Carolina yellow pine. Its eight large rooms were intact, as were the paneled wainscoting and the door and window trim. None of the original eighteenth-century hardware remained, although most pieces of 1835 vintage were still in place. The separate kitchen was in fair condition, but the dairy and office dependencies were off their footings, and a comprehensive restoration of these buildings was obviously necessary. There was enough of the carriage house remaining to measure and rebuild it as it was originally.

This farmhouse contains many unusual features, including double doors and doorways, marbelized mantels and baseboards, paneled dadoes and doors, and a gently rising staircase in the hall with marbelized risers. The newel-post, although large in diameter, is appropriate to the other interior architectural features of the house.

A number of exciting details survive on the exterior of the house. Most prominent is a beautiful cornice of dentil molding and below it two bands of

Front view of the Roberts-Vaughan house in Murfreesboro, North Carolina. Notice the balusterlike enclosure on the floor of the porch. Courtesy of the Murfreesboro Historical Association.

Rear view of the Roberts-Vaughan house with its appendages. Note the massive chimneys on the ends of the house and on the kitchen wing. Courtesy of the Murfreesboro Historical Association.

fretwork that add grace and charm to the entire cornice entity. The second-floor entrance (off the porch) is banded with vigorous moldings which set off the double door and its attractive sidelights. The remnant of a spider-web window survived in the left gable end and provided details of design for the replaced window. On the left and right side are two massive brick chimneys with deep shoulders. A few surviving shutters provided a pattern for replacements. The weblike baluster of the front porch also repeats the original pattern. The four massive columns of the front portico, along with the corner boards of wood, heighten the house's resemblance to a Greek temple.

All of the outbuildings have been authentically restored and include many charming features. A ventilation grill in the dairy house is particularly attractive. The separate kitchen building has a large chimney to accommodate the commodious fireplace within. The entrance to the kitchen is sheltered by a cantilevered overhang. An office and a carriage house complete the complex of restored buildings. A brick pavement surrounding the enclave serves a practical purpose and at the same time unites the group of buildings into a picturesque and cohesive unit.

Thus, this eighteenth-century North Carolina river port has taken a step toward its regeneration as a city. Proud of its past and hopeful of its future, other projects will follow to make Hertford County more attractive to visitors and residents alike.

Some idea of the diversity of North Carolina's rural economy can be gained from the statistics for the year 1868. At that time the major crops consisted of Indian corn and tobacco, followed by rye, oats, potatoes, and hay. Only small quantities of barley and buckwheat were raised. Two major additional crops, peanuts and watermelon, have been raised during the twentieth century.

The attractive cornice and weblike window in the left gable end of the Roberts-Vaughan house. Courtesy of the Murfreesboro Historical Association.

The dairy house and the kitchen at the Roberts-Vaughan house. Courtesy of the Murfreesboro Historical Association.

Marbelized risers on the main staircase in the Roberts-Vaughan house. Courtesy of the Murfreesboro Historical Association.

Marbelized baseboard and handsome mantelpiece in the Roberts-Vaughan farmhouse. Courtesy of the Murfreesboro Historical Association.

11 Georgia

The original conditions involved in the settling of Georgia differed in many respects from those in other colonies. An excerpt from the *Encyclopedia Perthensis*, Perth, Scotland, 1800, describes the circumstances as follows:

> The settlement of a colony between the Savannah and the Altamaha rivers was first proposed in England in 1732, for the accommodation of poor people in Britain and Ireland, and for the further security of Carolina (from the Spanish in Florida). Private compassion and public spirit conspired to promote the benevolent design. Humane and opulent men suggested a plan of transporting a number of indigent families to this part of America free of expense. For this purpose they applied to the king, George II, and obtained letters patent, dated June 9, 1732, for legally carrying into execution what they had generously proposed. They called the new province Georgia, in honor of the king who encouraged the plan.

A corporation was organized consisting of twenty-one persons who were to become the governing body for the colony, the leader being James Oglethorpe, one of its active promoters. The settlers were not only transported free of charges, but were supplied with whatever was needed to build houses and cultivate the soil. However, quite a few years passed before any of these people came to own the land on which they lived.

From the very start the projected colony was not a successful operation. The settlers were ill-prepared to till the soil, particularly in a climate that was so hot and different from the one they left. The colony finally began to prosper after the trustees recognized the errors in the regulations which they had established. In 1752 the trustees were removed from their governing position, the settlers were allowed to have custody of their lands, and slaves were permitted to be brought in to work the soil. Originally slaves and rum were banned, for they were believed to encourage indolence and drunkenness. John Reynolds was appointed governor of the colony, and a legislature was elected on a plan similar to procedures in other colonies.

Probably no colony was founded with a stronger intent to encourage farming than this one. A description of the allotments, which the prospective farmers received, appears in *Life and Labor in the South* by Ulrich B. Phillips:

> A few "gentlemen colonists" went on their own expense, and some carried servants; but the main bulk was on charity, each family received a town lot and a hut upon it, a garden plot nearby, and a small farm in the vicinity, a cow, a sow, tools, seeds, and sustenance until they could become self sustaining. The trustees provided grape vines and mulberry trees from a public nursery, and silk worms along with industrial instruction and copious regulation in the affairs of life.

It is interesting to note that in the 1929 edition of the *Encyclopedia Britannica* there are two drawings of farmhouses, presumably typical of those found in Georgia. One is a pillared mansion, similar to those built in the tidewater region, where crops such as rice, cotton, and indigo were raised. The other is a drawing of a disheveled hut, which was obviously on the other end of the economic scale of farmhouses.

Unfortunately, the author was not able to visit the far reaches of Georgia, his traveling being confined to the northern counties. The land being basically hilly, this area is not oriented toward agriculture, and few grand farmhouses are located here. The farmhouse pictured opposite was originally a log house, but it is now covered with clapboards. It is the Claude Simpson home in Jackson County, Georgia. Although originally one room, it now has two. It stands precariously off the ground, particularly the porch post nearest the camera. Although this house takes on a drab appearance in a black and white photograph, it has very rich color in both the chimney and the clapboards.

The chimney is made of both fieldstones and bricks. I was told that the large base area was built of fieldstones because they were free. Only the top or small portion was built of bricks, because they were costly. Most cabins in this area have roofs of sheet metal, which provide adequate and lasting protection. However, few of these cabins have been painted and, for that reason, the clapboards are deteriorating faster than the roofs. Under these conditions the clapboards weather to a beautiful, rich, dark brown, blending pleasingly with the landscape. On the other hand, the subtle red of the

There is a stone in the left chimney of this house with the date 1832. This is the oldest house visited in Georgia. It is located near Gainesville.

decaying bricks in the chimney and the earth colors of the stones form a perfect contrast. The aged owner of this cabin (it is now unoccupied) said she came to live in it on her wedding day, so it isn't over fifty years old.

The next small house was built in three parts, the first being the smallest and the central part of the house. The property consisted of 182 acres, most of which were planted in corn, hay, and cotton. The farm must have prospered at one point to account for the addition of the larger, refined front section. This part is comprised of a hall between two rooms, which must have substantially improved living conditions for the family living there. There is a chimney in only one room, it probably being the parlor, the other room a bedroom. This chimney is also built of fieldstones and bricks. It is

The Claude Simpson home in Jackson County, Georgia, originally was a log house. Appendages have been added to the front and back, and it has been covered with clapboard.

First-floor plan of the Claude Simpson home.

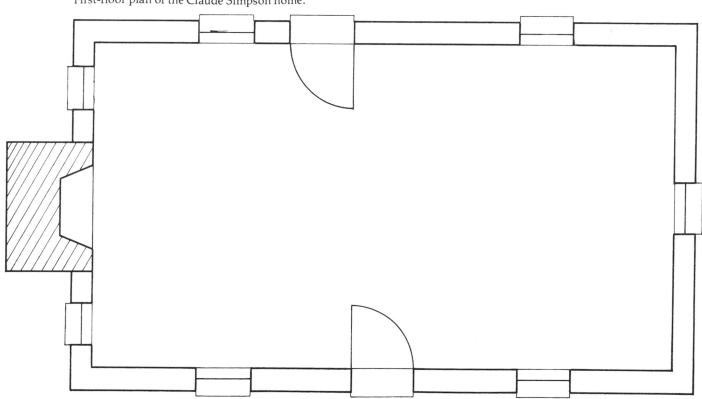

This small house located in northern Georgia was built in three stages. It is the residence of Katie Elrod.

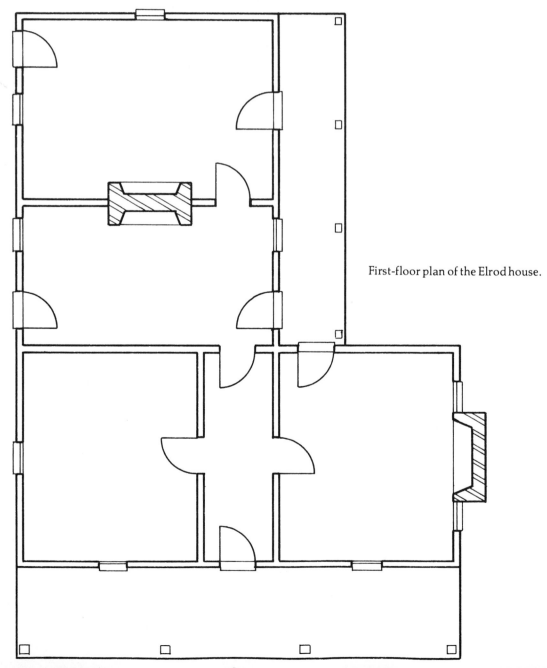

First-floor plan of the Elrod house.

also possible that stones were used because they were more heat resistant than bricks, for the bricks seem to be quite soft and would not have withstood the deteriorating effect of the constant heat very long. The stones have apparently held up very well. The front porch was probably constructed when the front portion of the house was added. Many of the houses in this area have front porches. This house also has a porch that was built along the back rooms of the house. Finally a summer or work kitchen was added at the rear of the dwelling. This appendage also has a fireplace, which kept the farm culinary work out of the everyday kitchen. This dwelling is presently occupied by the owner, Katie Elrod.

All the houses visited in Georgia were built in the nineteenth century. Another attractive farmhouse is owned by Mr. and Mrs. G. A. Kenimer and located in White County, Georgia. This house was also built in three sections, the last addition being made in 1872. The part to the right when facing the front is the oldest. The proof that it was built first is evident in the central hall, for there the old wall is still covered with the clapboards which were originally the outside of the house. In addition to the central hall there is another small one leading to the second floor from the last bedroom built as an ell, on the far left side.

There are four fireplaces in this large house, one in each of the two front rooms—a parlor and a bedroom. It has been pointed out previously that it was a common practice to have a bedroom on the first floor of farmhouses. In back of the front room on the right is a dining room, behind that a pantry, and beyond it a kitchen with a chimney terminating in the ceiling. This chimney was an outlet for a stovepipe from a kitchen range located there. Finally, on the far right side is a small room designated as servants' quarters. A spacious hall separates the old and the newer parts of the house, the front being known as a reception hall. Beyond the gently rising stairs is a back hall.

The distinctive local feature of the house is, of course, the double-tiered porches across the entire front. With balusters on the second floor, and none on the first, this arrangement has been found in many houses of the area and as a matter of fact, throughout the South.

In its day the farm was a very productive one. Various grains, beans, and peas were prominent field products. Later, these were augmented by crops of watermelon and fruits from a vineyard and an apple orchard. On a nearby knoll the headquarters of the Cherokee Indians was located, and in another direction there was a gold mine with four stamping mills. This is, in addition to its other fine qualities, a rich historical site.

A fine Victorian farmhouse located two miles south of Helen in White County is owned by the L. G. Hardman family. The house was built in 1870 by James H. Nichols, a druggist. The father of the family which presently owns the property was a bachelor when he bought it, completely furnished. It has a library that contains many old and important books and documents relating to the history of the community, especially about a nearby mill which ground the grain raised on the farm.

The G. A. Kenimer house has two large porches that extend across the entire front of the house. It is located in White County, Georgia.

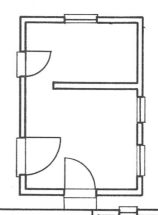

First-floor plan of the Kenimer house.

The L. G. Hardman house in White County, Georgia, is Victorian. It was built in 1870 by James Nichols.

The house is a grand example of Victorian architecture. It has a central hall with long stairs, their great length being necessary because of the high ceilings of the house. There is a fireplace in each room, and in each of the bedrooms a washbowl is installed in one corner. The one in the master bedroom is enameled in colors. All the doors are thick and made of walnut wood. Around the front door are panes of red and transparent glass.

The grounds are beautifully landscaped, the front lawn burgeoning with a half-dozen magnolia trees as high as the house. It appears that they were planted when the house was built. On the south side of the house stands a curious-looking building, which, upon inquiry, was found to be a Victorian greenhouse. Other buildings consist of several barns, a smokehouse, and a

The Victorian greenhouse at the side of the Hardman house.

separate kitchen. A covered walkway connects the kitchen with the main house. The barns have stanchions for one hundred Jersey cows, their milk being used to make butter, which was sold locally and also shipped to nearby cities. In the romantic words of a Victorian writer of *Health Resorts of the South* the site was described as follows:

> The dwelling is spacious and surrounded by broad piazzas, over which are entwined flowering vines, and here Capt. Nichols has gathered around him everything that makes life pleasant, a large farm, well stocked, rich fields, trained hounds, and plenty of game, fish ponds, a choice library, gas, pure spring water throughout, greenhouse, fountains, and nearby on a rise of land, shaded by beautiful oaks, the captain has erected a charming little church finished in natural woods from the trees of the forest of Nacooches Valley, comprising many different shades and colors which beautifully harmonize, and this gem of a church Captain Nichols has deeded to the trustees of the Presbyterian Church.
>
> "West End" comprises 2,600 acres, much of which is in virgin forest, beneath which are treasures of gold. . . . . The stables and outbuildings are commodious and conveniently arranged, the whole forming one of the most perfect country seats of the South.

Part IV
THE
OUTBUILDINGS

12 Springhouses

Springhouses have been an important part of the farm scene for a long time, although most of those existing today have survived from the nineteenth century. Extremely little has been written about them: one chapter on the subject appears in B. D. Halsted's *Barn Plans and Outbuildings*; another in *The Pennsylvania German Family Farm* by Amos Long, Jr.

Halstead points out that before a springhouse is built, a constant supply of cool water must be assured. The temperature of springwater at its source is usually in the mid-fifties. If the spring is located outside the springhouse, it must be cleared of all natural debris and protected by a wall enclosing it and a roof covering it. The water should then be piped to the springhouse, preferably at a height that will permit circulation of the water in raised troughs. Such an arrangement will eliminate much of the backbending required to manage the crocks and pans placed there to cool. If such a height cannot be attained, the water must circulate in channels below the floor level. The author has encountered several springhouses that had very small dry floor areas, the rest being covered with cool fresh water.

Many springs break out in the side of a hill, requiring that the springhouse be built against the hill to assure the utmost in quantity and freshness. After the water circulates throughout the masonry channels, it leaves the springhouse through a small outlet, purposely small to keep out straying animals. Some outlets were covered with an iron mesh or metal bars. While one springhouse was being photographed, a frog came out to see what was transpiring. The owner of the property informed the author that a frog in residence is evidence of good pure water.

The floors of springhouses were covered with stones or bricks and later with cement to provide solid footing for containers. Most springhouses were built

Interior of springhouse with elevated trough. Courtesy of *Barn Plans and Outbuildings* by B. D. Halsted.

Interior of springhouse, with low trough. Courtesy of *Barn Plans and Outbuildings* by B. D. Halsted.

Spring-, wash-, and smokehouse located on the John Johnson farm at Piqua, Ohio. Courtesy of the Ohio Historical Association.

of stone, a few of wood. If the structure was built of wood, a sizable base of masonry was required to prevent the wood from rotting. The room should permit walking without stooping and should be well ventilated; however, the louvers or other means of ventilating must not permit excessive hot air to enter. A ventilator in the ceiling is the most satisfactory location. Roofs were generally made of hand-split shingles and, in some cases, red tiles. In the Oley Valley of Pennsylvania one was found with a tile roof; it will, however, need repairing very soon. In recent years many of the oldest roofs have been covered with sheet tin or aluminum, much less attractive, but it does a satisfactory job. Although no springhouses were found performing their original function, many have been maintained with electric pumps, which force fresh water to all parts of the farm complexes.

Several houses were found with springs located in a corner of the cellar. Historians like to point out that this practice was followed to assure a supply of water, in case the place was under siege by Indians. Such a romantic need was probably unlikely; in actuality the location was largely a matter of convenience. As such, it was not practical or popular, for a damp cellar was apt to cause a damp house. One example observed by the author was isolated in the end of the cellar by a secondary wall of stone.

Many springhouses were built with a second floor, sometimes containing a fireplace, as well as a door and windows. These often served early settlers as shelters until more satisfactory residences could be provided. It was reported to the author that a certain politician was proud of the fact that he had been born in a springhouse.

Springhouse on the site of the ironmaster's house at Hopewell Furnace, Berks County, Pennsylvania. In the right end is a room with a huge fireplace for culinary work.

Springhouse with a red tile roof in the Oley Valley, Pennsylvania.

Two-story springhouse in Chester County, Pennsylvania. The pintles on the doorframe indicate that originally the door was in two parts, divided horizontally.

Stone springhouse with a grill over the window for ventilation, near Pottstown, Pennsylvania.

Springhouse on the Kiel farm near Catskill, New York.

A more logical use for the second floor was for the churning of butter. Space was required for the butter churn, and for the table on which the butter was washed, salted, and prepared for the market. Churns were either round vertical types or horizontal rotating barrel types. The barrel type had staves and hoops like a barrel, and within were a number of stationary arms, which were designed when the barrel was rotated to agitate the cream to form butter. Churns were often operated by hand, sometimes by sheep or dogs, and·in large-scale operations by horse power.

The churning required about an hour's time, after which a little cold water was added to make the butter "gather." A rocking motion also helped to make the butter gather at the bottom of the churn. A secondary product known as "buttermilk" was recovered from the churn and fed to the hogs. Today buttermilk is formed by chemical action and is not as tasty as the old-fashioned kind. After the butter and buttermilk were removed, the churn was cleaned by operating it with fresh water. Later the churn was placed upside down to drain and dry on a shelf outside the springhouse. This action signaled the end of a day's activities.

In the nineteenth century, Philadelphia butter had the reputation of being the best available; most of it, however, was made in Lancaster and Chester

The building in the right foreground is a large springhouse. The spring is enclosed by the wall between the two buildings. In the Oley Valley, Berks County, Pennsylvania.

counties. This superior butter was the result of the churn and also a device called a butter-worker, both located in the second floor of the springhouse.

The butter-worker was a round table as large as twelve feet in diameter, the top slanting inward and downward toward the center. About twenty pounds of butter were placed on the table at one time and were kneaded by a tapering, corrugated roller, fastened in the center, and moved around the outer circumference by an operator. As small amounts of buttermilk were worked out of the butter, they ran toward the center and were drained in a receptacle.

Later came another secret process, called "wiping the butter." A clean damp cloth was placed between the butter and the roller; this removed all the moisture that had not been previously squeezed out. This action produced a crisp waxlike butter, a quality it never seemed to lose. Finally, the butter was salted and placed in tin cans or firkins so that it could be cooled and made ready for market.

The butter was then weighed into smaller portions and stamped with a butter print appropriate to the size of the pad of butter. The most common motif was a sheaf of wheat, but more unusual ones contained swans, eagles, or motifs such as acorns and flowers.

Springhouse at the Gov. Thomas Worthington farmstead near Chillicothe, Ohio.

Brick springhouse near Chillicothe, Ohio. Courtesy of Dr. and Mrs. William Garrett.

Two-story stone springhouse in Loudoun County, Virginia.

Springhouse at the Hardman farm in White County, Georgia, has many ventilators.

While activities in the springhouse played a very important part in the weekly life of the farmer, all this work from milking to selling was relegated to the women and children. The men undoubtedly lent a hand, particularly in the winter, when their chores at the barn were at a minimum.

Springhouse built into a hill, with a frog in residence. Near French Creek, Pennsylvania.

13 Summerhouses

The concept of a separate small kitchen (house) on the farm may have had its origin in America when the original small house was replaced by a larger one nearby. The frugal farmer could not think of abandoning a former home, so in some cases, when the two buildings were attached, the original residence was used as a kitchen for the new house. If the two buildings were not attached, a small space separated them, similar to a breezeway between a modern house and a garage. There are numerous examples where this open space between the houses has been enclosed, thus creating an extra room. This procedure was followed at the Jacob Martin farmstead in Lancaster County, Pennsylvania. In this convenient location, Martin set up an office for administering the various business activities of a large working farm.

A variation of the summerhouse exists in the South, where a separate kitchen was built and used throughout the year. The mild weather of the South permitted such a convenient procedure. The heat and odors of the kitchen were kept entirely out of the main residence, on a year-round schedule. The best-known example of this procedure is found at the Governor's Palace in Colonial Williamsburg. A different version of the all-year kitchen is seen at Belle Grove near Middletown, Virginia, where a large kitchen is located in the basement of the house; however, it was moved to a wing when an addition to the house was made.

In a manner somewhat similar to that of Belle Grove, there were many summer kitchens located in the cellars of farmhouses in Pennsylvania and in the central part of Virginia, where many farmers from Pennsylvania settled. One cellar known to the author was divided into halves, one of which was kept dark and cool for the storage of foods and had an earthen floor, while the other half was used as a kitchen and had a floor of wide boards. This area also had a fireplace, several windows, an outside door, as well as one leading to the upper level of the house.

Summerhouse on the Jacob Martin farmstead, Lancaster, Pennsylvania.

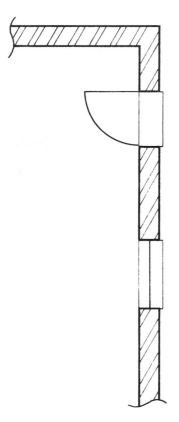
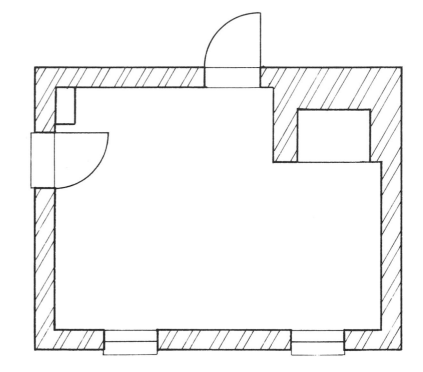

First-floor plan of the Jacob Martin summerhouse.

A variation of the summerhouse in the South is the summer kitchen. This one is located at the Hardman farm in White County, Georgia.

This summerhouse was very attractive at one time, having doors and windows similar to those found in the main house. It is located near Allentown, Pennsylvania.

Summerhouse near Taneytown, Maryland. It has a typical "Southern" chimney.

194

A very charming stone summerhouse with a bell tower at Colebrook, Pennsylvania. The bake oven is intact in the extension to the right.

This stone summerhouse, with its pleasing architectural details, is located on the East Berlin road, in York County, Pennsylvania.

A nineteenth-century summerhouse built of clapboards with a uniquely large chimney. Located near Millersville, Pennsylvania.

A brick summerhouse located near York, Pennsylvania. The chimney can be seen in the far left corner among the tree limbs.

The fireplace is no longer used, for a more satisfactory facility for cooking and baking became available in the early twentieth century, namely, a cast-iron cookstove. The smoke pipe for the cookstove was simply stuck into the flue, which carried the smoke away from the fireplace. The space around the smoke pipe was closed with a piece of sheet metal.

Such summer kitchens appear in farmhouses that were built against a hill, similar to the bank barns of southeastern Pennsylvania. Such a location kept them cool in the summer and quite warm in the winter. However, when cool weather came in late September, the culinary duties were moved to the main kitchen on the first floor of the farmhouse.

Summerhouses were built of stone, wood, or bricks, or perhaps a combination of two materials. Many of the ones built of masonry materials had window frames and doors made of wood, as well as the interior trim.

The roofs were usually a gable type with the ridge pole in the middle of the roof. Most of the original roofs were made of split shingles, which have now been replaced with sheet tin or aluminum. A few summerhouses have been maintained for uses such as farm workshops and for general storage purposes. A few with cellars are being used for food storage.

Some summerhouses have porches. The one on the farm where the author grew up had a wide porch, and at one side was a trough of fresh cool water flowing from a spring located on a higher level. The water was used in the daily work of the kitchen, but memory serves best in recalling that after dressing in the morning, one went to the water trough and filled a basin to wash one's face. This was a very positive way in which to awaken. Another trough was located in the cellar of the house, and in wintertime the daily routine took place indoors. The water, however, was from the same source. On the wall above the troughs was a row of nails for hanging four or five basins.

The main function of the summerhouse was to keep the heat of summer cooking away from the main house. The summer kitchen was made cooler by the openings on three sides, none being usually found on the end occupied by the fireplace. Windows were wide, in the style of the nineteenth century, and, of course, the door could be left open.

There, meals were prepared for the family and farmhands. All sat down to eat at the same time, except the mother and possibly an older girl, both being occupied with seeing that all the dishes were kept filled with food. After the evening meal was served, the men sat on the porch or in the yard while the women of the family washed the dishes. At nightfall most of the family went to bed. For the family this meant going into the main house, which was kept reasonably cool with closed shutters, those on the second floor having louvers to let fresh air circulate. The hired help slept in the attic or on the second floor of the summerhouse.

As for the construction of the summerhouse, it might be noted that they ranged from one floor to three. The main floor was used for cooking and meal serving and for heavier kitchen chores, such as soap making or cooking

This stone summerhouse has a bake oven attached and is located near Rawlinsville, Pennsylvania.

This summer kitchen with bell tower now serves as a bathhouse. Located at French Creek, Pennsylvania.

meat at the time of butchering. At butcher time the kitchen table was pushed aside, and a heavy four-legged table made of two- or three-inch planks was placed at a convenient spot for cutting and trimming meat. These tables are used today in a modern decor, for they are completely functional and have none of the frills found on some old furniture. They were heavy enough to have meat grinders mounted on them and have the appearance of being designed for the purpose they were used. Some of the meat was cooked in the fireplace or on the stove and stored in crocks with a layer of fat on the top.

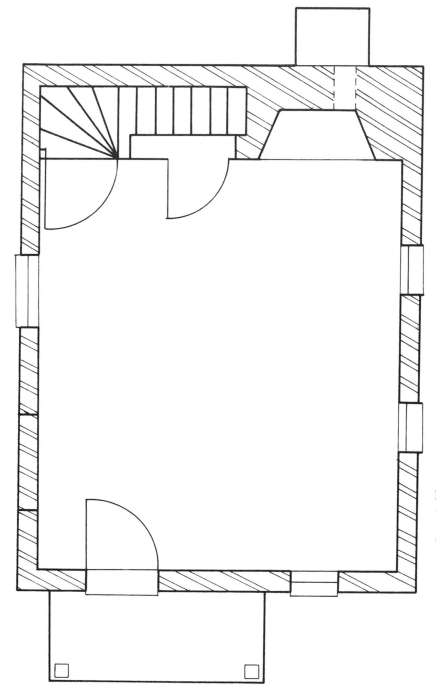

Floor plan of brick summerhouse with cellar entrance and bake oven on the right rear. Near Rawlinsville, Pennsylvania. See color plate.

Summerhouse with a fine bell tower near Millersville, Pennsylvania.

Victorian summerhouse, located near Harrisburg, Pennsylvania, with a very attractive bell tower.

Eighteenth-century summer kitchen with a Victorian bell tower. On the Fruitville Pike, near Lancaster, Pennsylvania.

Summerhouse originally built of logs, but completely encased with clapboards. Near Spring Grove, Pennsylvania.

Not all summerhouses have cellars, for usually the demands of a cellar were met when a second permanent home was built, which usually had a cellar under the entire house. However, one summerhouse was found with a beautiful vaulted cellar for winter storage of root crops and apples. There was an outside entry to the cellar, the door having a grill for ventilation except in very cold weather, when most of the grill was closed. The walls of the first and second floor were plastered. In reality, this structure could have easily served as a small residence. Since the main house is partially built of logs (but covered now), one would expect that the sophisticated summerhouse was built many years after the main house.

At least one summerhouse was found with a fireplace on the second floor. This floor was obviously designed as quarters for hired help or for the performance of light farm duties for which the area was adequate. The room was well lighted and a very pleasant place in which to live or work.

Two major appurtenances can be seen outside of the summerhouse, namely a bell tower and a chimney. Each bell tower is different and presents a charming appearance on the roof of a summerhouse. A length of rope or wire was dropped to the ground level in order that the housewife could conveniently ring the cast-iron bell. It was rung in times of emergency or to summon men from the field for meals. Many youngsters eagerly awaited the sound of the bell for more than one reason. The photographs show that there were considerable differences in the design of these bell towers. Their main attraction lies in the shape of the steeple and the openwork around the bell. Those of the Victorian era are particularly attractive because of the fretwork found on them. Unusual pride accounts for many having survived until today.

Certainly the fireplaces were an indispensable part of the summer kitchen. They were always built spacious enough to accommodate the large iron kettles used in the routine of farm work. The kettles were hung from a crane which could be swung outward over the hearth to be filled or emptied. The cooked meat was handled with a set of large culinary tools consisting of a skimmer, ladle, and fork. In rare cases a spatula completes the set. Some of these tools are profusely decorated and are eagerly sought by collectors of ironware.

Today many summerhouses serve as guesthouses on restored farmsteads or as artists' studios. They are a charming survival of the farm scene; it is hoped that their continued existence will enable future generations to get the "feel" of farm life in the eighteenth, nineteenth, and early twentieth centuries.

14 Bake Ovens

Because the American pioneers are known to have been remarkably resourceful people, historians are apt to attribute to them achievements which were not really theirs. The art of baking in an oven built in the wall of a fireplace was practiced for many centuries before the pioneers tried it.

By looking into the history of baking in the eighteenth and nineteenth centuries, it becomes apparent that little was baked in the pastry line except rolls and bread. Many kinds of bread were baked—the type being determined by the addition of ingredients, such as potatoes, rice, turnips, the tops and barks of gooseberry trees, holly gorse, and hawthorn. In the old days alum was added to wheat bread to make it white. And, of course, there was French bread. The ingredients of French bread are similar to those of other breads made from white flour, except that milk and butter are added, and apparently it has to be baked in a very hot oven.

In most areas on the Eastern seacoast, the oven was an integral part of the fireplace wall. The entire fireplace was built of masonry materials, either stones or bricks, and designed so that wood could be successfully burned and the cavity heated thereby. In the eighteenth century, fireplaces were very inefficient and were inclined to be large—more wide than tall.

In the back wall of the fireplace an opening was provided, possibly twelve inches in height and fifteen inches wide, which led into an oven that was made of masonry materials and entirely closed except for the opening into the fireplace. The opening could be opened or closed at will. These cavities varied in size, depending on the demands made of them. A family of ten naturally required a larger oven to bake a week's supply of bread than did a family of five. As a matter of fact, sometimes there were two ovens; however, they may have been used for baking two products rather than for the production of an enormous quantity of bread. A small oven was possibly two and a half feet in diameter; some were elongated but deeper. Ovens located in institutions were usually very large.

Bake oven built against an outside wall of the Brush house at Williamsburg, Virginia.
Courtesy of Colonial Williamsburg.

204

Outside bake oven in yard near a house west of Harrisburg in Cumberland County, Pennsylvania.

A beehive oven at the home of Leland R. Meyer at Spring Valley, New York.

Large oven facility, with wood-storage area in the rear at the Daniel Boone farmstead, Berks County, Pennsylvania.

The hearth, or the floor of the oven, was flat, as were some of the roofs, but most of the roofs were arched. A wooden frame was used to support the arch until the mortar was dry, after which the frame was burned. This was a practical way to remove the wood and hasten the drying process.

In New England the oven was an essential part of the fireplace wall, usually placed to one side, in order that it would be accessible when a fire was burning in the fireplace. The body of the oven was located within the masonry fireplace stack of the house, and normally, no part was visible except the opening. In Pennsylvania two practices were followed in installing ovens. One procedure was to have an opening in the back wall of the fireplace, as in New England, but the body of the oven was outside the wall of the house and was very evident to passersby. In this location, the oven had a roof to protect the masonry from the onslaught of rough weather. Another practice was to build ovens that were completely detached from the house and located at a convenient place in the yard, usually at the side or

Outdoor oven attached to outside wall of fireplace. At the Robert Carter kitchen in Williamsburg, Virginia. Photo courtesy of Colonial Williamsburg.

Outdoor oven showing a beehive top, near York, Pennsylvania.

Drawing of a combination bake oven and smokehouse, from *Barn Plans and Outbuildings*, by B. D. Halsted.

back. This procedure was probably followed to keep separate the activities of cooking and baking, but the location exacted severe penalties in the winter.

Halsted's *Barn Plans and Outbuildings* furnishes some clues regarding the construction of good serviceable outdoor ovens. First, a masonry wall is built of bricks, two courses thick and to a height of two feet. On the inner course oak planks were laid at least four inches thick. The full wall was then continued for another six inches in height, and the space between the planks was filled with mortar, on top of which was laid a bed of sand, fine coal, or wood ashes. On this nonconducting base the hearth for the oven was laid. Hard bricks were used, fitted close together, and bonded with mortar. The wood for supporting the dome temporarily was placed on top of the hearth, and the dome built over it. The outside wall was then continued several inches above the dome, and the cavity between the dome and the outer wall was filled with sand. After the oven was built, it was covered with a substantial roof. These ovens could retain heat for long periods and could be used for a century or more.

An alternative to building separate ovens and smokehouses was to combine the two. The advantages of such a procedure were to save money in construction costs, to use one fire to operate both facilities, and to provide an unusually dry space for smoking meat. There probably were some disadvantages, but the planners did not mention them.

As time passed, while methods of baking remained unchanged, improvements in the ovens themselves were taking place, particularly in New England. The earlier ovens had to be placed in the back wall of the fireplace, for most of them did not have smoke flues, and the smoke drifted out of the front opening and went up the chimney. Sometime, possibly in the late eighteenth or early nineteenth century, the oven was moved to the side of the fireplace, and often a separate flue was linked up to the main flue to heat the

Projecting bake oven at the rear of a mid-nineteenth-century farmhouse, near Millersville, Pennsylvania.

Bake oven in one of the outbuildings at Shirley, Charles City County, Virginia. Photograph by Haycox Photoramic, Inc. Courtesy of Shirley Plantation.

oven more efficiently. For this arrangement the fireplace hearth had to be extended beneath the oven, since ashes, which had formerly been raked on the hearth of the fireplace, now were raked onto the extended hearth and shoveled into an ash cavity under the oven. One oven located at the side of the fireplace had a special ash flue to poke the ashes down onto the main hearth of the fireplace. The discarded hot ashes were an excellent place to bake potatoes.

The operation of the oven was virtually an art in itself. One authority insisted that green wood be used, for it gave a very hot flame. Green wood could have been slightly dried by placing a small quantity within the oven after the baked contents had been removed. This procedure was an evident liability, for laying fresh hard wood on the hot hearth was liable to break up the masonry floor. Bread, of course, had no such effect; frequently a second load was put in after the first one was removed. The diminished heat required that the second load be exposed for a much longer time than the first. Beech wood was considered the best wood for heating an oven.

It was recommended that to build a fire one piece of wood be placed crosswise in the oven and that smaller sticks be rested on it. It is evident that the large crosswise piece acted as an andiron, providing a draft that allowed the other pieces to burn. Presumably, when the large piece was completely burned, the oven was ready for baking.

Determining the proper heat was also a crucial matter, and there seem to have been as many ways to do this as there were bakers. One suggests that a green leaf that turns black when put into the oven is a sign the oven is ready. This procedure posed a problem in the wintertime. Others recommended placing a small pile of flour at the entrance to the oven: If the flour turned black, the oven was too hot; if it was nicely browned, the baked goods were added. Another authority states that the correct time had arrived when the soot was burned off the roof of the oven. But the author believes that the real "pro" determined the correct heat by sticking his hand into the oven.

To quickly fill the oven the bread had to be conveniently placed nearby. In the house a table would suit the purpose. Most of the outdoor ovens needed a roof extending forward to shelter the baker and the baked goods in case of rain. Under this roof there were shelves for the baked goods, both before and after baking.

The bread was slipped into the oven with a flat, shovel-like peel. It had to be long enough to reach the remote areas of the oven. The largest loaves

Indoor bake oven, with door open, in the family kitchen of Van Cortland Manor House. Courtesy of Sleepy Hollow Restorations.

Bake oven in a summer kitchen at Palatine Bridge, New York. Courtesy of Mr. and Mrs. Willis Barshied.

were placed in the rear, for that was the hottest area, there being only a minimal loss of heat when the door was opened. Two options were open for baking smaller loaves or other pastries. One was to put them in the oven with the large loaves and remove them early. Or one could put the smaller pieces in later and remove all at the same time. Both procedures required that the oven be opened at least once during the process of baking, thus narrowing the choice to six of one and a half dozen of the other.

The delicacy of bread baked in one of these ovens is difficult to describe. The taste of hot brown crust that dripped over the edge of the pan, topped with a little honey, was well worth the trouble to get the two together. Of course the ingredients of the bread and the skill in baking it determined its taste. Although a week's supply of bread was baked, presumably on Friday, no preservative was added, and even when the supply was running low, it still retained its special flavor.

15 Root Cellars

In times past vegetables could be stored in a number of ways. A reasonably good and simple approach was to select a high point in a field or the yard and stack produce (turnips, cabbage, carrots, celery, etc.) on a pile six feet wide at the bottom and four feet high, sloping inward toward the top. The heap could be made very long, or separate piles could be made for different vegetables. They were covered with a foot of straw well compacted and finally with three to six inches of earth. The earth had to be well compacted to resist being washed away when it rained. At intervals of not less than six feet, pipes were inserted to aid in ventilating the buried vegetables. Some sweating did occur within the mound, and spoilage would follow if the mound was not properly ventilated. The mounds could be opened on a mild day to remove vegetables without harming the others left within. Large storage areas similar to the one described were used in Germany as late as World War II to store "cow beets." A German resident told the author that sometimes the cows had to share the beets with the populace in the last days of the war.

Another mode of storing root crops was in the cellar of farmhouses. Before furnaces were installed there, cellars were usually cool, dark, and damp—three conditions necessary for good storage. Loose soil could be laid on the ground floor of the cellar, and vegetables laid on top or "dug in." Celery kept well in this manner, and in addition it was blanched, making it crisp and very tasty. Potatoes were kept in the cellar until spring, and apples could be kept in the cellar well into the winter if kept in barrels or boxes.

A sizable number of Pennsylvania farmhouses had built in their cellars a room known as a cold or arch cellar. They were called arch cellars because many had a rounded arch as the ceiling, a mode of construction which was

A very primitive-type root cellar located near Willow Street, Pennsylvania.

A root cellar which is completely underground, located at Richboro, Pennsylvania.

A combination root cellar and springhouse, located at Colebrook, Pennsylvania.

sound and attractive. All of them were built of masonry materials (bricks or stones) with a straight wall at the sides possibly five feet tall, the balance of the construction being an arch. They ranged in size from a small one found in a summerhouse, which was about ten by twelve feet and seven feet tall, to a large one, found in a Victorian farmhouse, which was about fifteen by twenty feet, with a height of about twelve feet. The floor of this large room was about three feet below the level of the cellar floor. Care would have to be taken to make such a room watertight, or else the bottom of it would be filled with water, and the contents ruined.

Root cellar, partially underground, near Rawlinsville, Pennsylvania.

Root cellar on the grounds of Abbeyville Estate, near Lancaster, Pennsylvania.

Ventilation for the small cellar was obtained through a grill in the door. This arrangement was satisfactory, for the door was an outside entry to the cellar. Larger ones required more than one opening, which, again, had to be screened to keep unwanted insects and animals outside. Since openings are usually small, the room could be kept dark and damp. Storage included the usual vegetables and fruits; in addition, barrels of cider and vinegar were kept there.

Many such storage facilities were also built in barns; they served not only for the storage of food for the table, but for root crops fed to the animals as well. These were not finished as nicely as the ones located in the cellar of the houses, but they served equally as well. The author grew up on a farm which had such a facility in the barn.

If the farmhouse lacked an arch cellar or storage outside of the house was preferred, there was a reasonably good way to meet this demand. The procedure was to dig a hole or wide trench into the side of a hill, piling the displaced earth where it could be easily reached to throw back on top of the cave roof. If the ground was very firm, no side walls were necessary. A peaked roof of logs or heavy boards was built over the cavity with supports in the center to keep the roof from collapsing, with the weight of the ground thrown on top of it. The replaced earth had to be at least two feet deep and then covered with sod to keep water from seeping down to the wooden frame. Such seepage would in time rot the framework, and the roof would collapse.

Frequently provision for a door was made, the areas on each side being filled with additional boards or with masonry materials if a more permanent use of the facility was intended. The door had to be tall enough to permit entry without stooping. Often a manhole at the front was used—less convenient for entering, but better able to protect against frost than a full-sized door. The cavity was ventilated by inserting a pipe at the rear, equipped with a device to keep out unwanted insects and rodents.

The final word in cold storage on the farm was to build a fairly sophisticated cave in the yard, where stored fruits and vegetables would be easily accessible. The building of these involved digging a trench, usually into a hill, but not always, and building masonry walls and an arched roof. An example was found in Ohio, where the arched roof was built of blocks, designed for the building of a circular silo. By following the contour of the curved blocks in the roof, the cave was half the circumference of a silo. The facility was faced in the front with flat rectangular blocks used to construct the base of the silo.

Although the masonry roofs of such caves were made weathertight, it was additionally covered with earth and sod for insulation. The earth kept it cool in the summer and reasonably warm in the winter. This type was completely frost-free.

The doors for permanent cave cellars could be installed vertically, or a slanting bulkhead arrangement could be used, if the cave was completely

Modern building blocks were used to build this root cellar in Holmes County, Ohio.

Root cellar on the grounds of Shirley Plantation in Charles City County, Virginia.

Root cellar dug completely into a hill near Rawlinsville, Pennsylvania.

Entrance to a root cellar near Willow Street, Pennsylvania. The house and the root cellar are built into the side of a hill. The farmhouse is a typical example of a type built in Pennsylvania during the last half of the nineteenth century.

underground, as many were. Both types of entries are illustrated in the photographs of cave cellars. Sometimes meat was stored in cave cellars, but regardless of the contents, some provision was necessary to lock the entrance.

If orchards were located near a lake, or if another convenient supply of ice was available, some storage houses were built to be kept cool with ice placed in an appropriate location in the cave. Such storage facilities must be built especially for this procedure and are not as common as the aforementioned cave cellars. Of course, today, growers have storage plants cooled by modern refrigerating equipment.

16 Smokehouses

The preservation of meat and fish by smoking has been practiced by many ethnic groups for centuries. Primitive man devised a mode of smoking that was compatible with the foods of his culture. By the eighteenth century, the process had been refined to the extent that reasonably airtight buildings were erected near the farmhouse for this purpose. Although smokehouses have been used throughout the Eastern seaboard, most of the surviving examples are found in Pennsylvania and tidewater Virginia. In Virginia heavily smoked hams have been a delicacy and are still considered so today. A reasonably large meat processor in Lancaster, Pennsylvania, continues to smoke his meat in the old manner, although chemicals can now be used to bypass this long and tedious method of curing.

The chemical action involved in smoking meat in a smokehouse is to dehydrate the meat and improve its flavor by a slow application of wood-smoke which contains a high concentration of creosote. Meat has been smoked in a variety of ways, the only essential condition being an enclosed space where smoke can circulate from a smoldering fire. A novel plan is described in *Barn Plans and Outbuildings*, where a barrel is used instead of a smokehouse. A pit is dug partially under the bottom open end of the barrel and partially outside in order that the fire can be periodically fed. Holes are bored in the sides of the barrel near the top for the insertion of iron bars to hold the meat. The lid must be portable to allow convenient placement and removal of the meat within. The sketch of this facility shows a lid with a handle for easy action. It is suggested that the fire be fed with fine brush, corncobs, or hickory wood. Hickory wood was preferred in most cases for smoking meat.

Another mode of smoking meat without a smokehouse was to build a small cavity adjacent to the kitchen fireplace. In New England two such

Large stone smokehouse in the Oley Valley, Berks County, Pennsylvania. Note beehives in background.

facilities were found, one opening in the front of a fireplace jamb, the other in the side. Neither was commodious enough to hold more than a few pieces of meat. In Pennsylvania some farmers removed a few bricks from their chimney flue in the attic, permitting smoke to enter the area at the bottom and exit at the top. An adequate area was enclosed by a partition of wood, which through years of use became dark and greasy. Although no longer used, quite a few of these can be found in the countryside today.

The real business of smoking meat, however, took place in a small building built of wood, bricks, or stones, or a combination of these materials. The most primitive type found in this survey was one of logs located in Lebanon County, Pennsylvania. It is doubtful that a log structure would make a very satisfactory one, for it would have been difficult to make the walls completely airtight. Those of other materials were built with one or two stories, the taller ones having a revolving pole with arms in the center and steps to reach to the very top. There were also pulley arrangements for placing meat at points in a smokehouse that could not otherwise be easily reached. A minimum amount of draft for the fire could be managed by leaving a few bricks or stones out of the wall near the top of the structure. Meat was suspended on a hook shaped like an S, with the very sharp point piercing the meat and the other end (blunt) hanging over a bar or another hook.

Smokehouse on the Minor Bartlow farmstead at Hamilton, Virginia.

223

Round smokehouse constructed of stone and wood at the Pennsylvania Farm Museum, Lancaster County, Pennsylvania.

Although most smokehouses were built on level ground, some were built against the side of a hill, which was not a bad idea since such an arrangement permitted easy access to the house on ground level, while the top section could also be reached through a door on the opposite side and on the upper level. It was recommended that those made of wood be plastered on the inside to reduce the hazard of fire—another good idea, for many are known to have burned, with the complete loss of the winter's supply of meat.

In the ground floor of a conventional smokehouse a pit was dug to contain the fire. This pit was as deep as two feet, for it had to hold a sizable quantity of wood. Many farmers favored the use of green wood. It did not burn very fast, and also was thought to produce a desirable quality in the smoke. Because butchering was usually done in the winter, a fire was started before the meat was hung to prevent the meat from freezing. Since smoke could not penetrate a frozen ham, a preheated smokehouse was a necessity. It was also important that the meat did not get too hot. If this occurred, the fat oozed out of the meat and minimized the action of the smoke.

A small stone smokehouse at Hellam, Pennsylvania.

Smokehouse with a bell tower at Shirley
Plantation, Charles City County, Virginia.

Vestiges of a log smokehouse,
in Lebanon County, Pennsylvania.

226

A two-story smokehouse on the grounds of Wheatland, near Lancaster, Pennsylvania.
Wheatland was the home of President Buchanan.

A two-story stone smokehouse on the grounds of the Colonial Pennsylvania Plantation.

The building on the right is a smokehouse, the one on the left is a dryhouse. Located at the Quiet Valley Living Historical Farm near Stroudsburg, Pennsylvania.

Smokehouse of half-timber contruction, covered with clapboard in Holmes County, Ohio.

A double smokehouse with slate roofs near Reinholds, Pennsylvania.

Smokehouse at Belle Grove near Middletown, Virginia. The entry can be seen through the arched opening on the left.

A fine old smokehouse near Silver Springs, Pennsylvania.

A sophisticated plan for a smokehouse is found in the book *Barn Plans and Outbuildings.* This one is built of bricks about eight or ten feet high and has a circular roof. About eighteen inches above the floor level a series of iron bars was placed near enough to each other so that slabs of bacon could be placed on them for smoking. About eighteen inches under the roof another set of iron bars was installed from which hams and large pieces of meat were suspended. In addition, iron hooks were inserted on the inside of the masonry wall for hanging meat.

One interesting smokehouse was found at the Pennsylvania Colonial Farm, near West Chester, Pennsylvania. This was a two-story affair built into a hill. The bottom area was used for smoking meat, and many old meat hooks had survived in the walls and rafters. A curious chimney of wood conducted the smoke from the lower room through the upper room and the roof, its bottom end being charred by long exposure to smoke. It is thought that the second floor, reached through a door on the higher level, was used as quarters for farm help, the area being large enough for several beds and other pieces of furniture.

In most smokehouses the meat was hung above the middle, for there the smoke gathered before it seeped out through the apertures provided for it. The biggest pieces were hung at the top. The length of time for smoking varied with the size of the meat and the intensity of the fire. With a vigorous production of smoke small pieces could be processed in a few days; large pieces often required a week. Many farmers claimed to have evolved special techniques over the years, which are known only to them. Most were able to produce a superior product; producers today often advertise their products as "old country ham."

Smoked meat should not be eaten immediately upon removal from the smokehouse. Thirty to sixty days are recommended for the perfection of taste. If the meat is stored for a matter of months, it should be carefully wrapped in a lightweight cloth, this procedure being followed by some producers today. The meat should be stored in a well-ventilated room, with precautions to keep it out of the range of rodents.

Sometimes the smokehouse was used for storage for an indefinite time. If this was done, locking the smokehouse was a necessary precaution. There are in existence antique locks, known to have been used on smokehouses.

17 Privies

After discussing most of the outbuildings connected with farmhouses, one finally comes to privies. They obviously cannot be bypassed, and one writer about farm buildings maintains that they are the most important of all. At certain times one would happily accept such a statement as the truth.

Perhaps the first problem, particularly for the uninitiated, is to define the word *privy*. After looking in dictionaries, it is found that they are very evasive about the matter. The first dictionary solved the problem in its own way by not including the word. Another dictionary defined privy as "a latrine." The next logical step was to look up the word *latrine*, only to discover that "a latrine is a privy." Another dictionary was very informative by saying that a privy "was a necessary," however, there was no definition for "necessary." Finally, another dictionary solved the problem by noting that a privy was "an outdoor toilet." That statement obviously settles the matter.

One of the first problems in building a privy is to determine its location. In New England some are known to be an appendage to the house, but in Pennsylvania they were usually built in the backyard. Then the distance is a matter between odor versus convenience. The solution varies with each farm site.

After the location is selected, the next problem is to select the material of which it should be built. Most of them are built of wood, either vertical boarding with wide cracks for ventilation, or clapboards, which are virtually airtight. One must decide whether they want snow in the winter or the prospect of great heat in the summer. A few are built of brick or stone, and these are elegant types, usually found with dwellings of either of the two materials. Wooden ones are usually painted to match the color of the house, the color of the trim is also a repeat of the house treatment.

A privy located in Holmes County, Ohio. It is hoped that this one is no longer in use. It has a floor of concrete.

This privy, also no longer used, is located near Gainesville, Georgia.

A decorator has touched the windows of this privy and added shutters and window boxes. Located near Douglassville, Pennsylvania.

Some privies have modern conveniences. This one has an electric light. Located in Berks County, Pennsylvania.

This privy, with heart cutout in door, is located near Allentown, Pennsylvania.

This privy, also no longer used, is located in Massachusetts.

After deciding upon the material, one is confronted with the shape the building should be. These are tough architectural problems. Not having found any octagonal or round ones, the only choices left seem to be either square or rectangular. The final decision must be based on the need, namely, will it be a one- or two-seater. If a two-seater is needed, the obvious answer is a rectangular shape, otherwise it should be square.

In any case, the problem of the height of the seats must be reckoned with. In case there are many heights to be accommodated, an average must be struck; however, with growing children the average will constantly change. Perhaps the solution is a three-, four-, or five-seater. One was found in Ohio with two seats the same height. The use of such a facility poses a difficult social problem. No inquiry was made about the solution.

Provision must also be made to fasten the door on both the inside and the outside. Care must be taken so that the fastening facilities do not function at unwanted times. Cases have been known where the outside functioned while the occupant was on the inside, and a more alarming emergency is for the inside retainer to function while the person is on the outside.

There is also a serious matter in ventilating the building. Traditionally there are cut-outs in the door such as hearts, half-moons, diamonds, et-cetera. These seem to be very inadequate, since they might only indicate in which wall the door is located. That fact is important to know. Of course many have windows, and presumably they can be opened or closed as the occupant wishes. A few have elaborate windows which seem to be installed permanently.

Then there are matters of interior decor. For example, the floor might be covered with linoleum. This material is very satisfactory for it can be scrubbed each Friday when general housecleaning is done. Maybe the color should be coordinated with that of the exterior. However, none have been found that were painted in the interior. A more elegant treatment might be the use of a braided rug, discarded from household use. This might also be color-coordinated. Rugs are not as satisfactory as linoleum, since occupants often have muddy shoes. One floor visited was made of cement, along with the stools which had "bought" seats. It is obvious that all kinds of variations are found.

In the old days the privy was a depository for obsolete mail-order catalogues. They have been replaced with a modern holder for a roll of toilet tissue.

The scarcity of privies causes one to believe that they are slowly going out of style. After all, a modern bathroom is more convenient and comfortable.

Part V
FARM MUSEUMS

18 The Pennsylvania Farm Museum

The Pennsylvania Farm Museum was the brainchild of two brothers, Henry and George Landis. They were longtime residents of Lancaster County, Pennsylvania, however Henry spent considerable time outside the county. He had a rather checkered career. He was a graduate of Lehigh University and worked as an engineer in various positions. He was the editor of several magazines, including one called *Plain Talk*, of which he was the founder. In 1924 he retired to the family home in Landis Valley and devoted his full time to the farm museum.

The life interests of George were different from those of Henry. George's major hobbies were collecting firearms and hunting big game. He hunted deer, bears, foxes, and wildcats in his favorite hunting ground, Clinton County, Pennsylvania. When he was a boy of fifteen he bought his first pistol and rifle. He soon decided to specialize in Kentucky rifles and was an avid participant in shooting matches.

Although the Landis brothers are long departed the museum bears the imprints of both men. They were regular attendants at county auctions in Lancaster County, and it is obvious that they were discriminating buyers. The decorative arts and farm equipment were Henry's major concern, and he is responsible for the collection of decorative ironware, copper, and brass, including a very charming still. Also for the pewterware, Fraktur, quilts, coverlets, woodenware, china, glass, and many other artifacts.

George is responsible for the fine display of firearms at the museum. There are examples of Kentucky rifles, muskets, pistols, and various objects concerned with trapping. There are two rifle benches and some boring bars used to bore rifle barrels. George was an expert mechanic; he repaired guns and cleaned all of those in his collection. He particularly enjoyed putting old guns into shooting condition.

Victorian farmstead on the grounds of the Pennsylvania Farm Museum.

Both men were involved in buying farm equipment. There are implements for "working" ground, for seeding, and for harvesting. Possibly the most attractive display in the farm area is a huge Conestoga wagon, surrounded with spare parts such as ax holders, tar buckets, and a variety of chains.

A series of workshops are displayed in the "Yellow Barn." There the visitor can see the tools of the tinsmith, blacksmith, coppersmith, potter, and so forth. A special building is devoted to crafts involved in the making of cloth. There are spinning wheels and looms, and competent craftsmen to demonstrate them. The ongoing development at the museum today is the construction of additional farm buildings and the refurbishing of those originally on the site, including three farmhouses. All the houses are attractively furnished with appropriate furniture.

On the edge of the museum grounds a new grouping of settlers' buildings has been erected, consisting of a barn, farmhouse, springhouse, and bake oven. The house and barn are duplicates of original log buildings in Pennsylvania, the barn having a thatched roof. A fire is usually kept in the kitchen fireplace, and on occasion, food is prepared there. A fine and usable bake oven is an appendage to one of the other farm buildings.

Two major events are held yearly on the museum grounds. In the spring a Craft Day is held, with many local craftsmen demonstrating their skills. In the fall, there are Harvest Days (Saturday and Sunday) when apple butter is boiled, cider is pressed, and various other activities can be enjoyed.

The Pennsylvania Farm Museum is operated by the Pennsylvania Historical and Museum Commission. It is open throughout the year but is closed during some of the major holidays.

19 Quiet Valley Living Historical Farm

Some farm museums have been going concerns for many years, others are relative newcomers. From a release of the Quiet Valley Living Historical Farm it is learned that in 1958 the Wicks family bought a farm in the foothills of the Pocono Mountains, three and a half miles from Stroudsburg, Pennsylvania, and a little more than one mile from Route 29, a spur of Interstate 80.

For the past eight years informal tours for school groups have been conducted from May until mid-June. Continuous tours during the summer have been open to the general public in this busy and growing resort area. Groups are limited to twenty persons. Family groups on a holiday or wide-ranging vacation trip are the most frequent visitors. A descriptive account by Wendy Mazer states:

> Quiet Valley Living Historical Farm is a Pennsylvania German farm homestead, a unique living farm, which has been restored on its original site for its historical, educational, and accompanying aesthetic and moral values. The farm-sized museum is the original seventy-two acre farm homestead established by a German immigrant family of humble origin, whose name appears in early records as Zepper, Depper, Dieper, or Topper. This family put down their roots in 1765 and kept the farm in the family until 1913. When the Wicks family acquired the farm in 1958 almost nothing had been changed. They began to fulfill a dream. Starting with the idea of establishing a "living museum" that will give today's generation a living contact with the heritage of their country's past, this public spirited family, including the younger Oilers of the next generation, has established a unique tourist attraction in northeastern Pennsylvania.

The Wicks had been students of the good and simple life, with special interest in the natives of this area and in thrift and ingenious ways of making what they needed from what they had. The purchase of the farm spurred their interest into restoring and rebuilding activities. In the summer of 1963, Quiet Valley, a living farm museum, was opened to the public; in 1967 it was incorporated. Visitors in the spring and summer of 1971 amounted to 10,000 for that year.

The present buildings consist of a bank barn, farmhouse, bake oven, smokehouse, dryhouse, washhouse, icehouse, and a "granny house." There is a new headquarters building rebuilt of logs from a site in Bangor, Pennsylvania.

Young girl "charging" a bake oven at the Quiet Valley Living Historical Farm. Photograph by Bryden Taylor.

The functions of most of the outbuildings in a self-sustaining farm have been discussed elsewhere in this survey. However, because this survey is basically interested in farmhouses, special mention should be made of the one at Quiet Valley. The house is described as having a cavelike kitchen, small and dark with a natural clay floor. The room is dominated by a great fireplace, which served for heating, lighting, and cooking. There is a cold room, surrounded by earth on three sides, which has an even temperature of fifty degrees Fahrenheit. It was used to store fruits and vegetables produced on the farm, in addition to vinegar and wine.

The usual addition was made to the house by building a second floor over the first. This was used principally as a work and storage area until a third story was added. The third floor was a sleeping area for the children and provided dry storage for strings of apples, dried pumpkin slices, and homespun bags of dried fruits and vegetables. Corn, beans, and sunflowers were suspended in baskets where they could be frequently inspected for damage from insects and rodents.

Furnishings of the house were meager, made mostly of wood in a very primitive design. There were wooden plates, bowls, and spoons, and bottles, ladles, as well as bowls made of gourds grown in the kitchen garden.

The granny house which stands near the original house was built to accommodate older members of the family, who were squeezed out of the big house by a growing family. They contributed work to the farm complex as they were able, and could give advice on any problem that perplexed the youngsters. This arrangement of houses is not unique to this farm; there is also a granny house in the Pennsylvania Farm Museum, and in other locations throughout southeastern Pennsylvania.

A visit to the farm is an inspiring experience. There a group of dedicated people are spending their energy to continue a life-style which has disappeared from the American scene. It gives visitors an insight into an older way of life, and it is hoped that it will entice some of them to return to it.

20 Colonial Pennsylvania Plantation

The Colonial Pennsylvania Plantation is a living historical farm museum, located in the Ridley Creek State Park at Edgemont, Pennsylvania. It lies between Philadelphia and West Chester, being closer to West Chester. The project has been under way for several years, but there is evidence of considerable progress and much promise for the future.

The history of this farm starts with the purchase of a 300-acre tract of land by Thomas Duckett in 1686. In 1720 Joseph Pratt I bought it, and for four generations it was owned by the Pratt family. In the late 1700s the Pratts operated a dairy farm on the site, and it is this era that the present staff is trying to simulate.

The intent of the farm staff is not to create a stabilized facility, but rather one that grows as money becomes available for its development. The brochure describing the project explains this concept:

> We have a dual purpose: we are a living history museum, and a museum in the making. By living as colonials we strive to answer questions about colonial American folklife. As we find these answers the farm changes constantly, and this farm is more like a process than an end product. The things you see are really experiments in American folklife and, as the experiments yield results, life on the farm will change and develop into something neither books nor archaeology alone can tell us.

The goal of the staff members is to not only recreate the farm life of the late eighteenth century, but to have visitors and volunteers participate in the growth. The staff deals with long-term projects such as refurbishing the springhouse, constructing fences, and renovating the interior of the farm-

Farmhouse on the site of the Colonial Pennsylvania Plantation.

house. This process goes on steadily and is hardly noticeable on a day-to-day basis. The visitor can participate in such immediate activities as feeding the livestock, helping in the harvest, or assisting the cook at the open fireplace.

There are vestiges of many buildings on the site, some having a high priority to be reconstructed so that they may become a functioning part of the farm property. The springhouse is high on the list, for since the Pratts operated a dairy farm, the springhouse was very important to them for cooling milk and as a cold-storage area for other beverages and food. It was also the source of pure clear water, a commodity essential to the practical operation of the farm facility.

Another building which could probably be used as is, is the smokehouse. It, like many of the others, is built of stone, which partially accounts for its survival in excellent condition. It stands off to one side of the house, where it could be conveniently reached, but not in one's view of the property as seen from the front of the house. The roof line of this building was changed a long time ago, but otherwise it remains virtually as it was built. It is believed that the second floor was used at one time for storage, at other times as the sleeping quarters for hired hands who were working on the farm.

Particular attention is paid to a building now called a workshop. Few of these have survived elsewhere, which is strange, considering the fact that it was an integral part of many farms. The brochure of the museum describes this building:

> Of all the farm buildings, this one clearly marks the center of men's work. This workshop served a number of functions, lending itself to blacksmithing, carpentry, tool repair, storage, and heavy leather work. The smithy's shop produced all the iron work needed on the farm—nails, harness rings, hinges, chains, latches, horseshoes, bolts and nuts, kitchen forks and spoons. . . . Copper and tin work would probably be done by a traveling "tinker," but it was not unusual for a farmer and one helper to produce the rest of the metalwork for the farm.

Considerable importance is attached to the farmer's garden, for it was the major source of food throughout the summer and winter. The brochure tells that vegetables, herbs, and medicinal flowers were grown there. Among the vegetables were lettuce, rutabagas, turnips, beets, carrots, beans, peas, onions, parsnips, leeks, cabbage, corn, and melons. (Tomatoes were thought to have been posionous.) These vegetables were eaten fresh in the summer and preserved for winter use by drying, pickling, or burial in a root cellar.

Visitors are made to feel very welcome here, and considerable time is expended in telling them the goals of the project. Children can pet goats and sheep as they roam in the yard and can witness any major farm activity that is going on at the time of the visit. The staff is dedicated to the project at hand, and with this involvement, the project will move along smoothly. An interesting descriptive brochure is available with the layout of the buildings on the site, as well as another map showing the location of the museum in relation to nearby highways and towns.

21 The New York Historical Association and the Farmer's Museum

The headquarters of the New York Historical Association and the Farmer's Museum is located at the edge of Cooperstown, New York, a sleepy little town of Victorian houses, white fences, trim green lawns, and a lake that is the source of the Susquehanna River. The Fenimore house is filled with valuable examples of folk art, its large barn is crammed with tools and artifacts of country living, and the Lippit farmhouse is an example of one built in New York 175 years ago. The Association sponsors seminars in the summer that are concerned with events and activities of the past.

The Lippit farmhouse owes its beginning to Joseph Lippit of Warwick, Rhode Island, who decided in 1793 to seek a home in upstate New York. He chose a site in Hinman Hollow, six miles south of Cooperstown. Returning later with his bride, he built a New England–styled house, which was probably the only style he knew. In the center was a large chimney stack with three fireplaces on the first floor. There was a small hall inside the front door, as well as a staircase which led to the second floor. In the front portion of the house were two large rooms, a kitchen and a parlor. In the rear were two bedrooms, a buttery, one bedroom for the parents of the family, another for guests. The second floor provided room for additional bedrooms as well as for storage.

The house had a normal complement of openings, the windows on the first floor having nine panes over six. The same arrangement is found on the second floor. The door was framed with simple moldings, and there was a transom to cast a little light into the front hall.

In 1952 this charming house was moved to the Village Crossroads on the museum property. Along with a barn and outbuildings it forms an important complex of farm buildings, such as one would find in many parts of New York State. The outbuildings were moved from Westmoreland, New

The Lippit farmhouse at the Farmer's Museum at Cooperstown, New York. Photo by
Mild V. Stewart. Courtesy of the New York Historical Association.

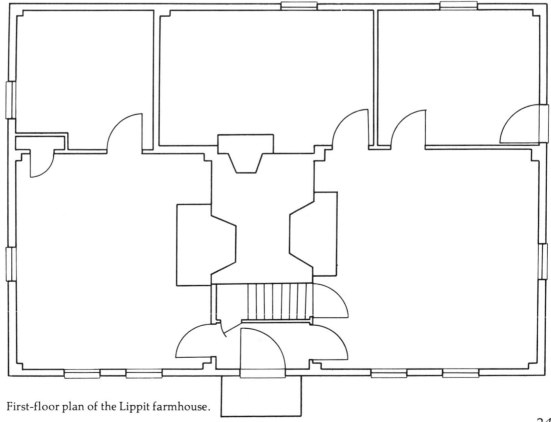

First-floor plan of the Lippit farmhouse.

York. They serve to protect the farm animals not only from the hostile winter weather, but from predators as well.

The house is furnished with furniture typical of the period, some a bit older, some a bit more recent. Much of the furniture was made of local woods by New York craftsmen. None of it is very elegant, but all of it exhibits a substantial quality appropriate for farm use. Bedcovers and other textiles are indigenous to the area. The stoneware is from the Hudson Valley, it being an important accessory for several farm operations.

The following excerpt from a museum publication explains the daily schedule of farm activities:

> Like many exhibits in the Farmer's Musuem, the Lippit farm is in actual operation throughout the year. Every day the animals are fed, the cows milked, and the barnyard chores completed. In the farmhouse ladies on the museum staff skim milk, churn butter, make cheese, tend the kitchen fire and, using old recipes, bake breads and cookies. On quiet days in the winter they make candles in the ancient manner—dipping, dipping, and redipping as the bayberry wax slowly fattens the wicks. They boil down kitchen fats, just as the frontier wife did using homemade lye to make soft soap. During the growing season the field is cultivated with old implements drawn by oxen or horses. . . . Here are the smells of the past—the manure and hay and straw in the barns and sheds, the burning wood in the fireplace, the herbs drying from the rafters, the spicy pomanders, the homemade soap, the cheese aging on the counters and the ginger-bread pungent fresh from the bake oven.

The author vividly recalls seeing sheep and lambs wandering on the museum grounds, and a fine pair of oxen, docile, strong, and beautiful. It is a pure delight to visit the Farmer's Museum at Cooperstown.

22 The National Colonial Farm

Each living historical farm is different from the others in one way or another. The very fact that they are situated on sites with varied geographical features points to a diversity of goals and ways to attain them. Fields and buildings are common to all; the degree of emphasis placed on their resources account for their difference in farm patterns. One has a furnished farmhouse that is open to the public, another has a modest house that is not open to the public.

At the outset of this discussion of the National Colonial Farm it should be noted that the farmhouse, although it is occupied by the farmer, is not a showpiece of the farm. The following brief description of the farm is taken from its brochure.

> The National Colonial Farm is an agricultural–Historical Museum project of the Accokeek Foundation. Located on the Potomac River opposite Mount Vernon, the farm provides an appropriate setting for the exhibition and demonstration of agricultural methods, crops, and livestock of a modest Tidewater farm of the mid-eighteenth century.
>
> Specific objectives to be carried forward as resources and opportunities allow.
>
> 1. CROPS: Tobacco, corn, cotton, flax, small grains, beans, squash, potatoes, melons, berries, and other small fruits.
>
> 2. FARM ANIMALS: Horses, oxen, dairy and beef cattle, sheep, hogs, chickens and other poultry.
>
> 3. WATERFRONT: A Colonial dock for the river ferry, eventually to be run for foot passengers from Mount Vernon and Fort Washington. Development of fisheries including shellfish and water fowl.

Winding road from the barn to the house at the National Colonial Farm.

4. WOODLAND: Conservation of the "waste" and woods upon which the Colonial farmers were dependent, including deer, semi-wild swine, rabbits, squirrels, and other small game, in addition to the then plentiful wild turkeys and other wild fowl.

5. DOMESTIC LIFE: A farmhouse, outbuildings, farm gardens, orchards, and similar related uses.

6. RESEARCH: Continuing genetic research on crops and such trees as the American chestnut.

This recital of objectives seems to include every activity that could be considered a legitimate goal of a living historical farm museum. The author, while visiting the farm out of season, as it were, observed the achievement of several of these objectives. There is a complex of farm buildings consisting of a barn, corncrib, sheep shed, workshop, and a laboratory building in which the farm office is located. The house on the property is a new one, designed to be similar to a house on a small mid-eighteenth-century farm.

Fields are cultivated to advance scientific research, as stated in the objectives. Horses grazed in the fields enclosed with old type "snake" fences. There was little "spit and polish" about the farming operation; it looked real and rugged.

The brochure further states that development of the National Colonial Farm has proceeded slowly but steadily since 1958. Frances P. Bolton, president of the Accokeek Foundation, and all others associated with the farm are anxious to share with the public the results of their work. However, it must be recognized that what will be seen is "work in progress" and, therefore, only a part of what is ultimately projected. Visitors' hours are 10 A.M. to 5 P.M., from June 1 through Labor Day; special groups may be admitted at other times by appointment.

23 The Carroll County Farm Museum

Although there is an educational motive in back of every farm museum, none states it more clearly than the Carroll County Farm Museum at Westminster, Maryland. This institution came into being when a county poor farm ceased to exist in 1965. At that time the six residents of the institution were moved to other quarters, and the farm museum was born.

A farm museum was a very logical use for the site and the buildings. Started in 1958, it was a working farm; the produce and the animal products were used in feeding the residents. A full complement of farm buildings was built when the farm first became operative. This includes a large house of thirty-two rooms, animal pens, several barns, a springhouse, smokehouse, blacksmith shop, machine shed, etcetera. There are objects of furniture such as a corner cupboard, cradles, stoves, a canopy bed, and an Eli Bentley clock, which was made in nearby Taneytown sometime between 1781 and 1822. It is the intent of the museum that these pieces should demonstrate a way of life rather than pose as outstanding examples of antique furniture.

The interpretation of the museum is directed toward the daily life of the farmer. It is explained that the entire family rose early in the morning, the men and boys going to the barn to feed the horses and the cattle, the mother and the girls staying in the house preparing a giant breakfast (by modern standards). The food consisted of sausage or hot cakes, fried ham, gravy, hominy, fried potatoes, biscuits, apple butter and jelly, and of course, coffee. Rarely eggs or cereal.

Throughout the spring, summer, and fall, the men worked in the fields planting, cultivating, and harvesting crops. In mid-summer grain was cut and shocked and later taken into the barn for threshing, an operation in which the grain is separated from the stalks. The grain was stored in a granary (a small compartment in an end of the barn), and the straw stored in the mows for bedding animals. In the fall the corn was cut and shocked until an appropriate time for husking. The husks were removed manually from the ears of corn, which were then thrown on a pile in the field to be later collected and stored in a corncrib. It was a very picturesque sight to see corn shocks and piles of corn lying in the open fields.

Through the winter months the women of the family continued to milk cows every morning and evening, this being a year-round procedure. If the men were not busily engaged otherwise, they would help with this daily chore. The women mended clothing or made new ones, made quilts from odd patches left from household sewing, and sometimes a community quilt was made by each person contributing a patch and helping to sew the various parts together.

Throughout the winter men had vehicles to repair, sagging gates to support, and harnesses to repair.

The museum literature notes that by the time the children were twelve years old, they could do most of the work done by adults. The girls learned to cook and sew, while the boys learned to plow and harness a horse. Their school year was short, so they could help with important work to be done on the farm.

Finally, the brochure points out that

> life was simple but good. Money was scarce, but so were the needs for it. Work was hard and hours were long, but the weariness that came from it was satisfying. Farm life produced happiness, excitement, knowledge, responsibility, and fulfillment. . . . For just a little while return to the relaxed atmosphere on a Carroll County Farm of the late 1800s.

The Carroll County Farm Museum is open weekends and Holidays from 12 noon to 5 P.M. During July and August it is open Tuesday through Friday from 10 A.M. to 4 P.M. The museum is always closed on Sundays.

24 Fruitlands Museum

The Fruitlands Museum, located at Harvard, Massachusetts, is unique among farm museums for instead of fields and gardens, the countryside is filled with orchards, as the name implies. Their brochure describes Fruitlands as:

> an historic, early eighteenth century farmhouse where Bronson Alcott established in 1843 a community under a new social and religious order known as the Con-Sociate Family. Now a museum of the Transcendental movement, it contains memorabilia of the leaders—Alcott, Emerson, Thoreau, Margaret Fuller, Lane and others.
>
> The buildings considerably pre-date the Fruitlands community's occupation so various aspects of life on an early farmstead are illustrated with furnishings and equipment common to the times. An attractive feature is a kitchen display, a full collection of culinary and old-time household gear in use during the Colonial Federal period of the house, long before the establishment of Bronson Alcott's New Eden.

The furnishings of this house are interesting, for they were updated as time and fashions passed on. Such an arrangement makes a visit both interesting and informative. The other museums on the site are the Shaker House, American Indian Museum, and the Picture Gallery. Many of the examples in the Picture Gallery fall into the category of folk art, which is very popular today.

The farmhouse at Fruitlands Museum.

Bibliography

Barrows, John A., and Waterman, Thomas Tileston. *Domestic Colonial Architecture of Tidewater Virginia*. New York: The DeCapo Press, 1968.

Bradford, William. *The History of Plymouth Colony*. Roslyn, N. Y.: Walter J. Black, Inc., 1948.

Craven, Wesley Frank. *The Southern Colonies in the Seventeenth Century*. Austin: University of Texas Press, 1949.

Encyclopedia Perthensis. Printed for C. Mitchell & Co., Perth, Scotland, 1800.

Frangiamore, Catherine Lynn. "Shirley Plantation in Charles City, Virginia." *Antiques*, February 1973.

———. "Shirley Plantation Journals." Unpublished manuscript.

Frary, I. T. *Early Homes of Ohio*. New York: Dover Publications, Inc., 1970.

Gilborn, Craig. *The Reliance on Tradition*. Columbus, Ohio: Charles E. Merrill Books, Inc., 1969.

Green Springs Historic District. Historic Sites Survey, Office of Archaeology and Historic Preservation, National Park Service, 1974. Unpublished document.

Halsted, B. D. *Barn Plans and Outbuildings*. New York: Orange Judd Publishing, Inc., 1909.

Hutslar, Donald. *Ohio History*. Columbus: The Ohio Historical Society, vol. 80, nos. 3 and 4, Summer/Autumn 1972.

Jenni, C. A. *The Niklaus Joss Letters*. Original printing in German. Translated by C. Richard Beam. Bern: 1833.

Jester, Annie Lash. *Domestic Life in Virginia in the Seventeenth Century*. Virginia 350th Anniversary Celebration Corporation, 1957, booklet no. 17. Distributed by the University of Virginia Press, Charlottesville, Va.

"John Cogswell's Grant and Some of the Houses Thereon, 1636–1839," *The Historical Collections of the Essex Institute*. Vol. XXVI. Salem, Mass.: 1940.

Kauffman, Henry J. *The American Fireplace*. Nashville, Tenn.: Thomas Nelson, Inc., 1972.

Kelly, J. Frederick. *Early Domestic Architecture of Connecticut*. New York: Dover Publications, Inc., 1967.

Lathrop, Elsie. *Historic Houses of Early America*. New York: Tudor Publishing Company, 1927.

Long, Amos, Jr. *The Pennsylvania German Family Farm*. Breinigsville, Pa.: The Pennsylvania German Society, 1972.

Luce, Gladness Wharton. *Historic Houses of Springfield, Vermont*. Springfield Art and Historical Society, n. d.

Nicholson, Arnold. *American Houses in History*. New York: Castle Books, 1965.

Phillips, Ulrich Bonnell. *Life and Labor in the South*. Boston: Little, Brown and Company, 1929.

Reynolds, Helen Wilkinson. *Dutch Houses in the Hudson Valley before 1776*. New York: Dover Publications, Inc., 1965.

Rivinus, Willis M. *Old Stone Work in Bucks County*. Doylestown, Pa.: Bucks County Historical Society, 1972.

Rodabaugh, James H. and Mary Jane. *Schoenbrunn and the Moravian Missionaries of Ohio*. Columbus: The Ohio Historical Society, 1971.

Rouse, Park, Jr. *Tidewater Virginia in Color*. New York: Hastings House, Publishers, Inc., 1968.

Rupp, I. Daniel. *History of Lancaster County*. Lancaster, Pa.: Gilbert Hills, 1844.

Rutman, Darrett B. *Husbandmen of Plymouth*, Boston: Beacon Press, 1967.

Schlebebecker, John T., and Peterson, Gale E. *Living Historical Farms*. Washington, D. C.: United States Printing Office, 1972.

Schoepf, Johann David. *Travels in the Confederation*. Translated by Alfred J. Morrison. Philadelphia, Pa.: William Campbell, 1911.

Schwartz, Marvin D. *The Jan Martense Schenck House*. Brooklyn, N. Y.: The Brooklyn Museum, 1964.

Waterman, Thomas Tileston. *The Dwellings of Colonial America*. Chapel Hill: University of North Carolina Press, 1950.

Waterman, Thomas Tileston. *The Mansions of Virginia*. Chapel Hill: University of North Carolina Press, 1946.

Wertenbaker, Thomas Jefferson. *The Founding of American Civilization, the Middle Colonies*. New York: Charles Scribner's Sons, 1938.

Weslager, C. A. *The Log Cabin in America*. New Brunswick, N. J.: Rutgers University Press, 1969.

Willich, A. F. M. *The Domestic Encyclopedia: Or, a Dictionary of Facts and Useful Knowledge*. Philadelphia: William Young Birch and Abram Small, 1803.

Worthington, Sarah. *The Private Memories of Thomas Worthington, Esq.* N. d.

Zell, T. Elwood. *Zell's Popular Encyclopedia, A Universal Dictionary of the English Language, Science, Literature, and Art*. Vols. I and II. Philadelphia: 1871.

Zeisberger, David. *Diary of David Zeisberger, a Moravian Missionary among the Indians of Ohio*. Translated from the original German manuscript and edited by Eugene F. Bliss. Cincinnati, Ohio: 1885.

MUSEUM BROCHURES

The Colonial Pennsylvania Plantation. Edgemont, Pa. 19028.

Morton Homestead. Administered by the Pennsylvania Historical and Museum Commission.

The National Colonial Farm. An Agricultural-Historical Museum Project of the Accokeek Foundation, Inc.

Pennsylvania Farm Museum. Administered by the Pennsylvania Historical and Museum Commission.

Piqua Historical Area. John Johnston Farm Buildings, Restored Section of the Miami and Erie Canal, Canalboat General Harrison, *Historic Indian Museum*, Ohio Historical Society.

Quiet Valley Living Historical Farm. R. D. #2, Stroudsburg, Pa.

Schoenbrunn Village. Ohio.

Visit the Restored Roberts House Circa 1790, an Adaptive Restoration in Murfreesboro, North Carolina.

Welcome to the Carroll County Farm Museum.

Index